FOR ORGANS, PIANOS & ELECTRONIC KEYBOARDS

E-Z PLAY TODAY
363

ACHY BREAKY HEART
AND OTHER COUNTRY CHARTBUSTERS

Y0-ASV-693

2 ACHY BREAKY HEART
(a.k.a. Don't Tell My Heart)
BILLY RAY CYRUS

7 BILLY THE KID
BILLY DEAN

10 BOOT SCOOTIN' BOOGIE
BROOKS AND DUNN

14 DALLAS
ALAN JACKSON

18 GONE AS A GIRL CAN GET
GEORGE STRAIT

26 I FEEL LUCKY
MARY-CHAPIN CARPENTER

22 I SAW THE LIGHT
WYNONNA

31 MIDNIGHT IN MONTGOMERY
ALAN JACKSON

36 NEON MOON
BROOKS AND DUNN

40 THE RIVER
GARTH BROOKS

46 SACRED GROUND
McBRIDE & THE RIDE

50 SHE IS HIS ONLY NEED
WYNONNA

68 STRAIGHT TEQUILA NIGHT
JOHN ANDERSON

58 TAKE A LITTLE TRIP
ALABAMA

64 THERE AIN'T NOTHIN' WRONG WITH THE RADIO
AARON TIPPIN

71 Registration Guide

ISBN 0-7935-1857-1

Hal Leonard Publishing Corporation
7777 West Bluemound Road P.O. Box 13819 Milwaukee, WI 53213

E-Z Play ® TODAY Music Notation © 1975 HAL LEONARD PUBLISHING CORPORATION
Copyright © 1992 by HAL LEONARD PUBLISHING CORPORATION
International Copyright Secured All Rights Reserved

For all works contained herein:
Unauthorized copying, arranging, adapting, recording or public performance is an infringement of copyright.
Infringers are liable under the law.

E-Z PLAY and EASY ELECTRONIC KEYBOARD MUSIC are registered trademarks of HAL LEONARD PUBLISHING CORPORATION.

Achy Breaky Heart
(a.k.a. Don't Tell My Heart)

Registration 5
Rhythm: Rock or 8-Beat

Words and Music by
Don Von Tress

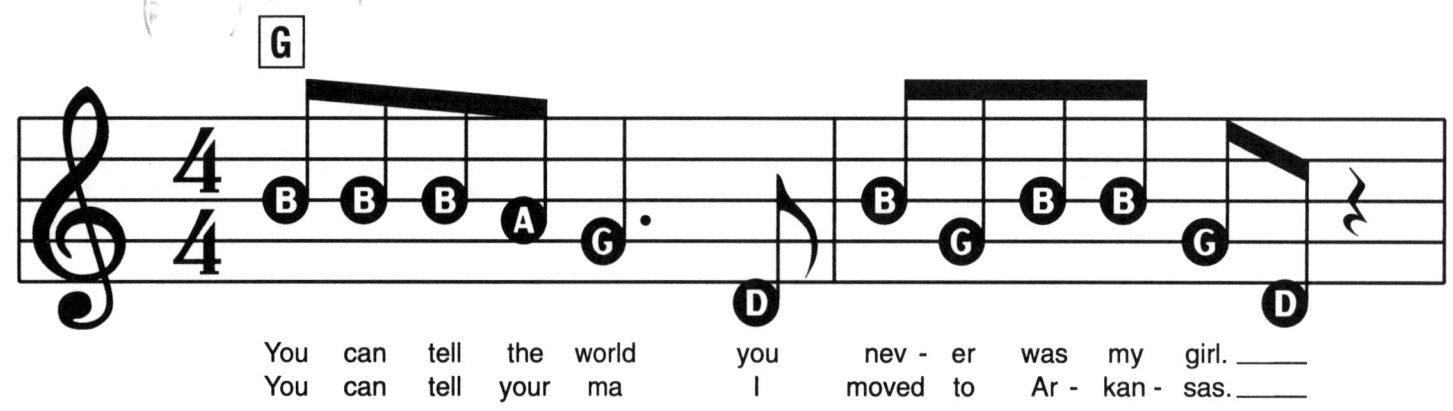

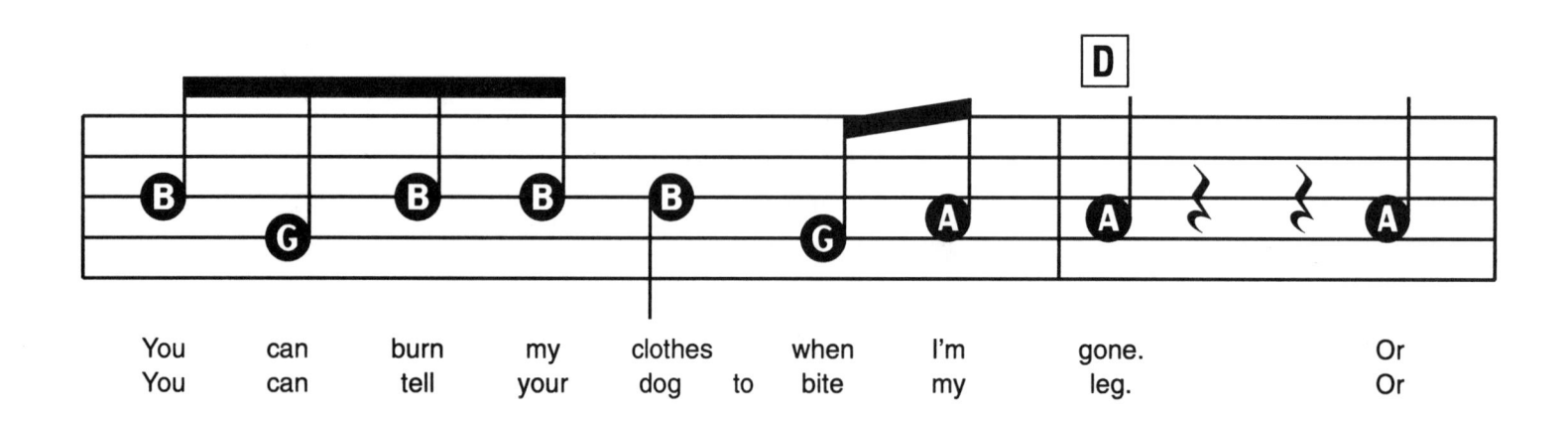

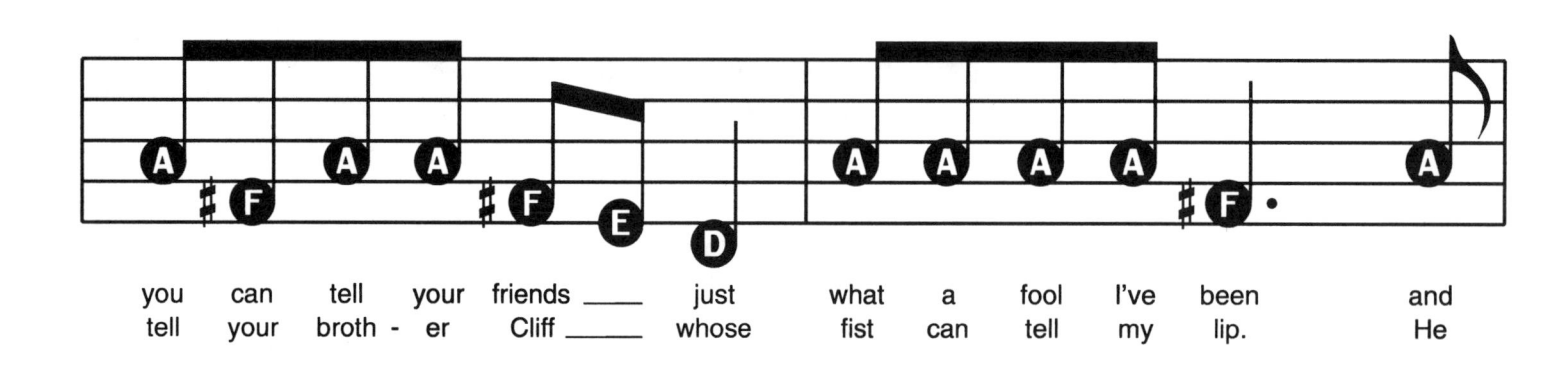

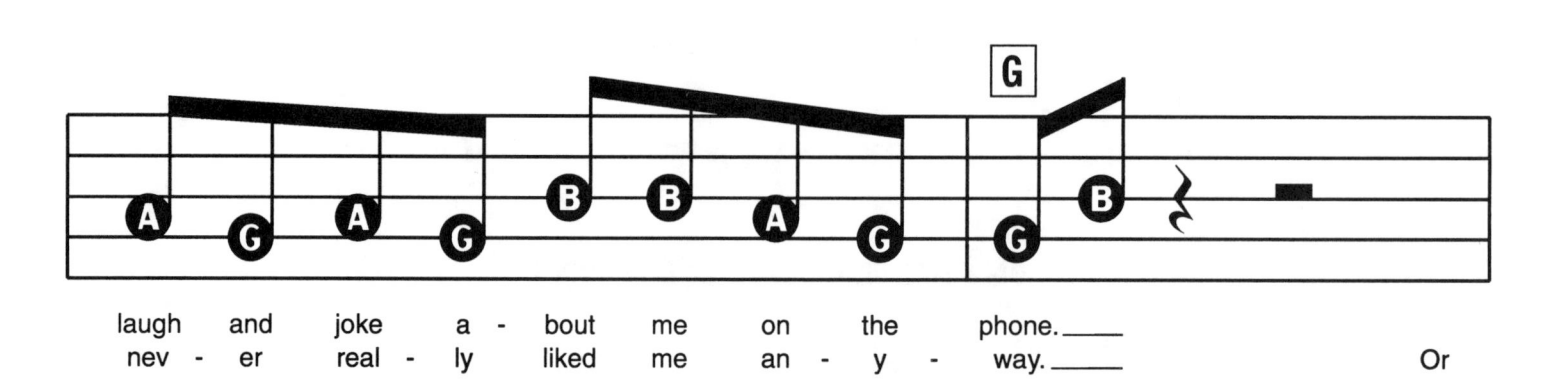

You can tell the world you nev-er was my girl.
You can tell your ma I moved to Ar-kan-sas.

You can burn my clothes when I'm gone. Or
You can tell your dog to bite my leg. Or

you can tell your friends just what a fool I've been and
tell your broth-er Cliff whose fist can tell my lip. He

laugh and joke a-bout me on the phone.
nev-er real-ly liked me an-y-way. Or

ßCopyright © 1991 Millhouse Music
All worldwide rights controlled by Songs Of PolyGram International, Inc.
International Copyright Secured All Rights Reserved

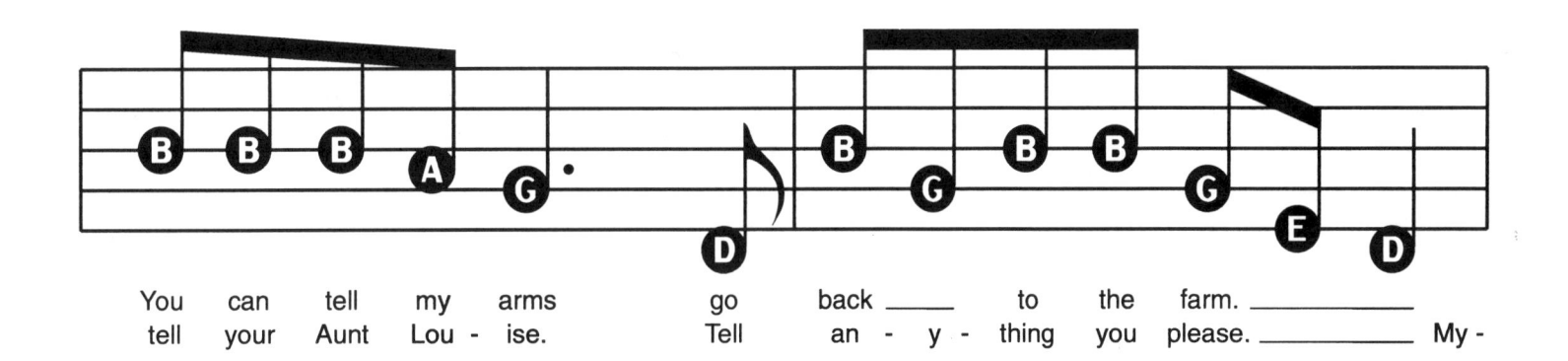

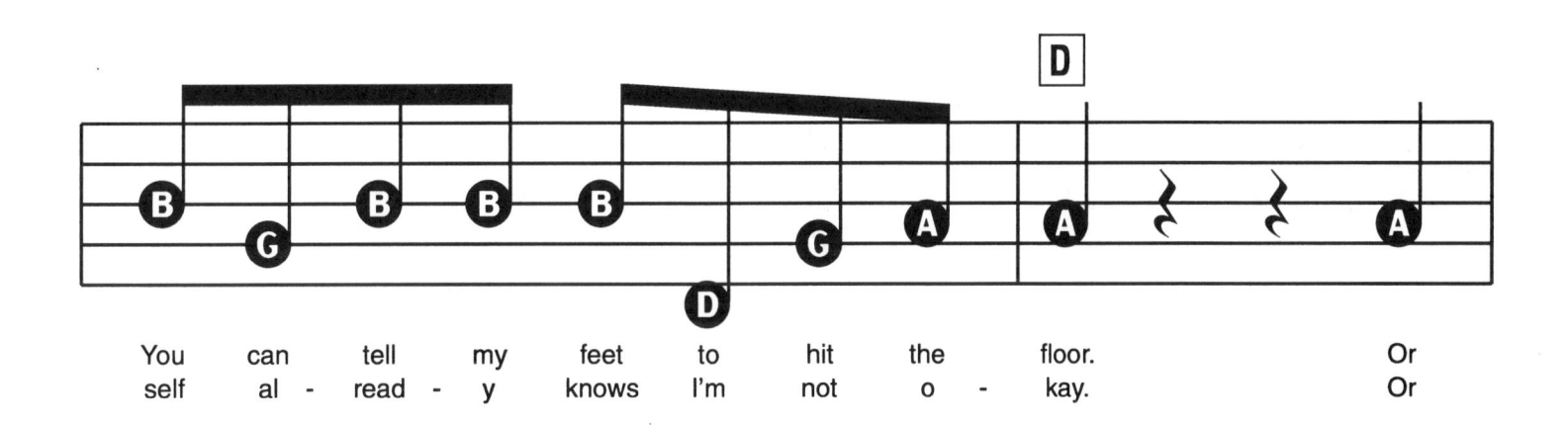

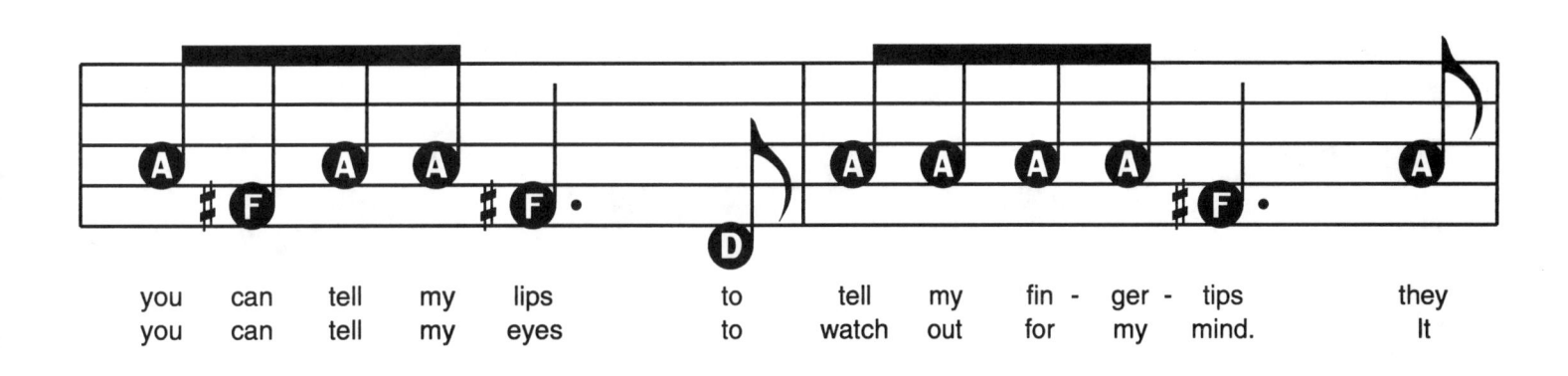

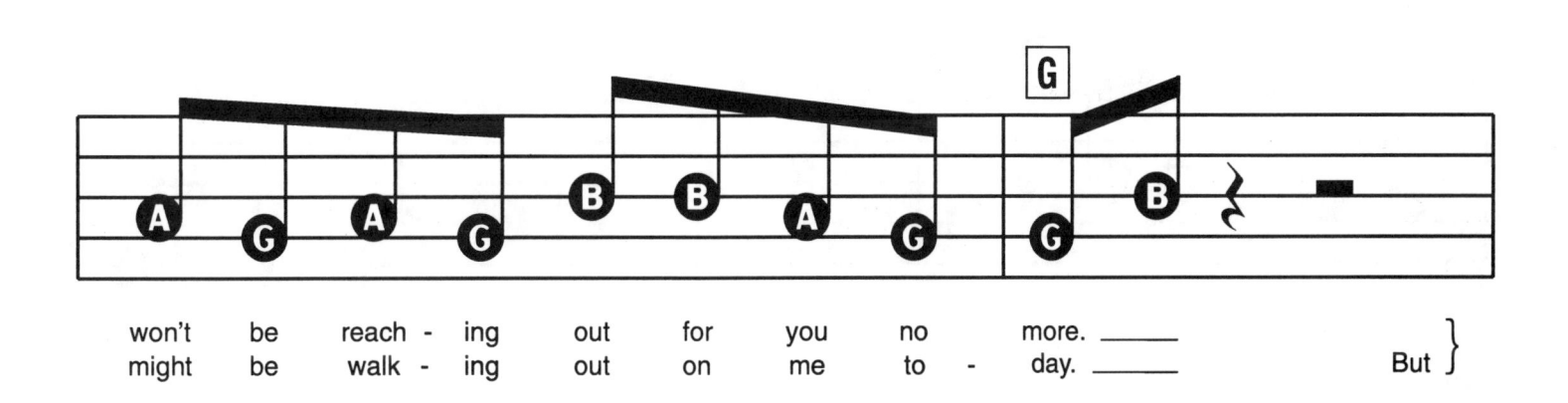

You can tell my arms go back to the farm.
tell your Aunt Lou-ise. Tell an-y-thing you please. My-

You can tell my feet to hit the floor. Or
self al-read-y knows I'm not o-kay. Or

you can tell my lips to tell my fin-ger-tips they
you can tell my eyes to watch out for my mind. It

won't be reach-ing out for you no more.
might be walk-ing out on me to-day. But

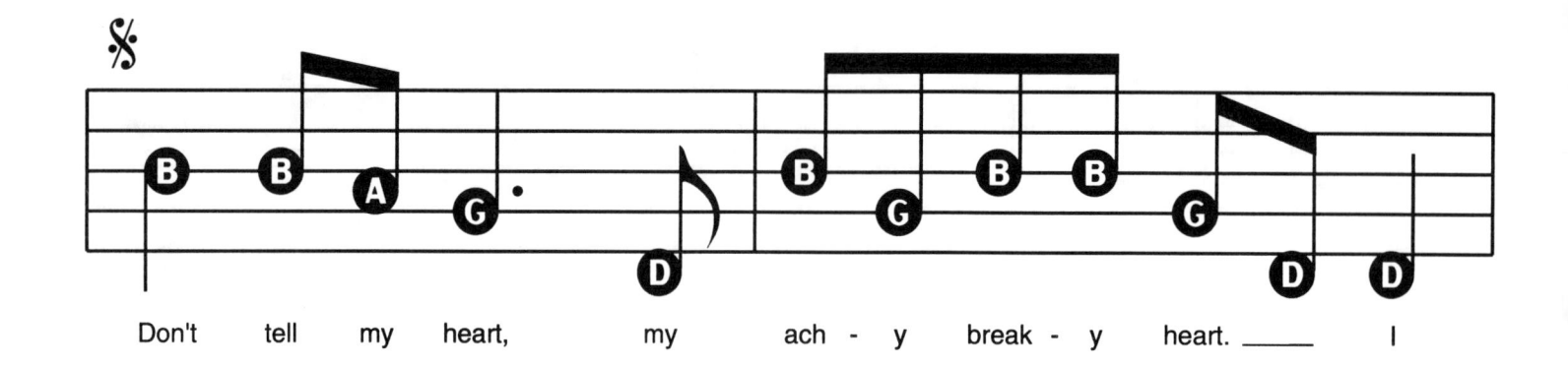

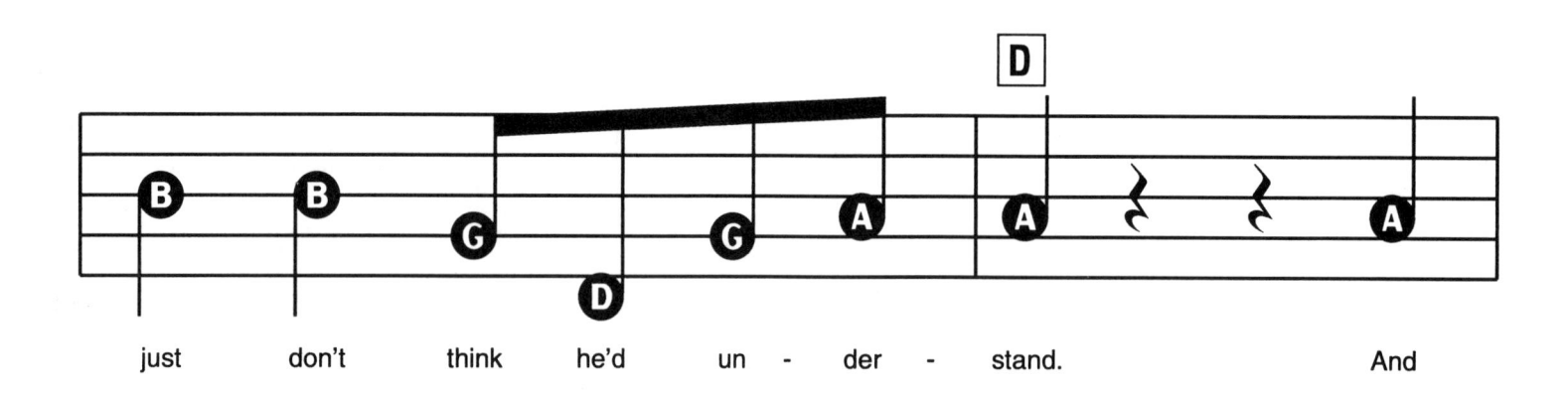

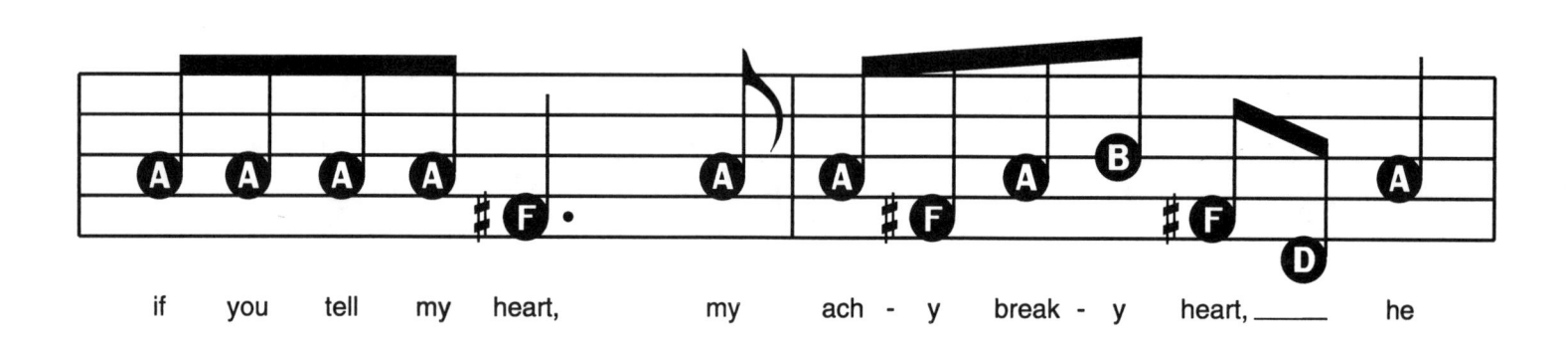

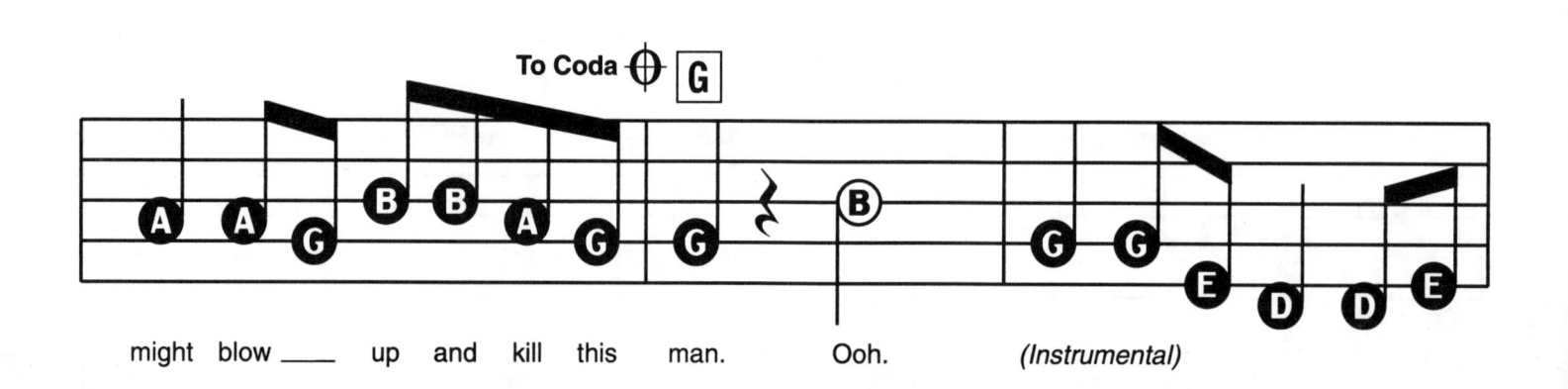

Don't tell my heart, my ach-y break-y heart. I just don't think he'd un-der-stand. And if you tell my heart, my ach-y break-y heart, he might blow up and kill this man. Ooh. *(Instrumental)*

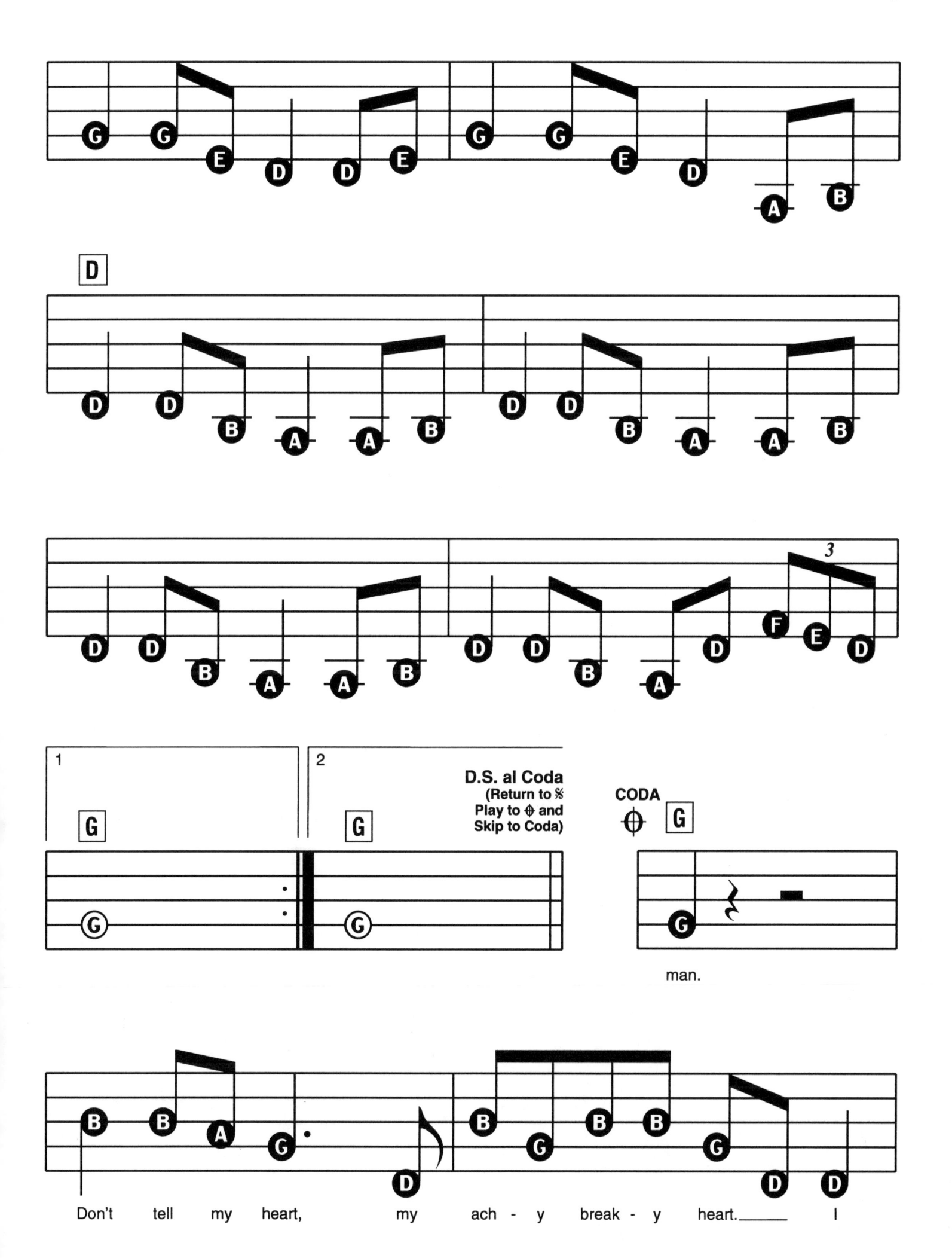

Don't tell my heart, my ach-y break-y heart. ___ I

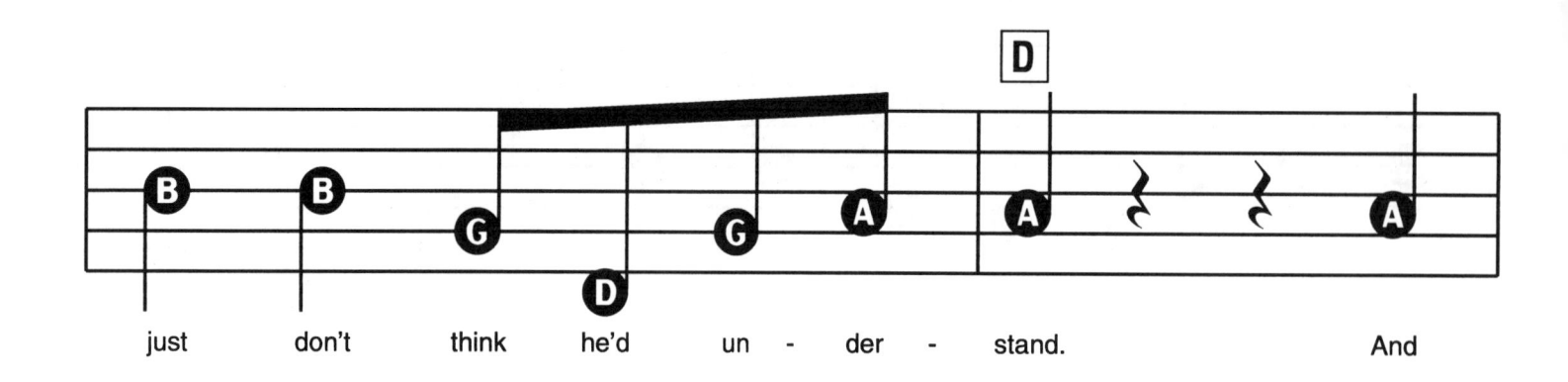

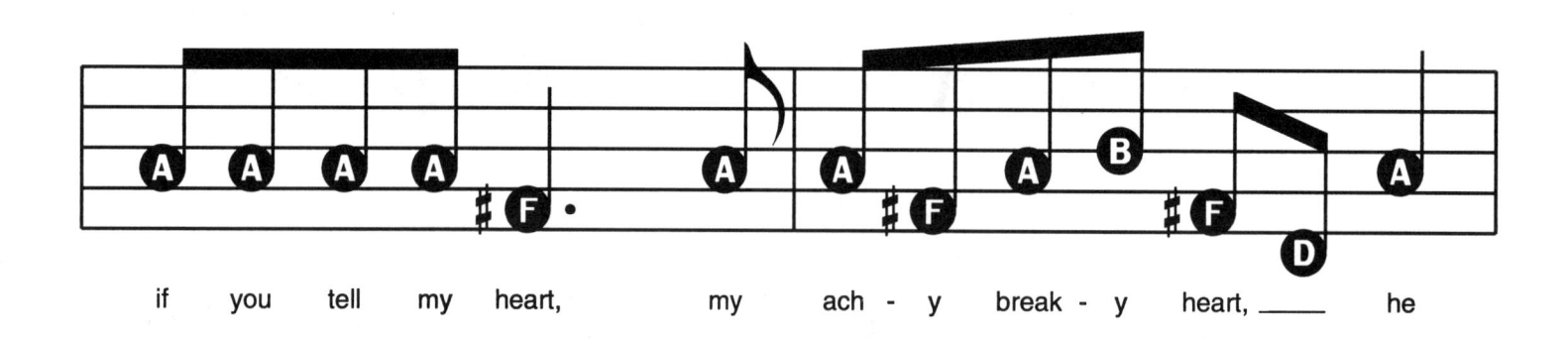

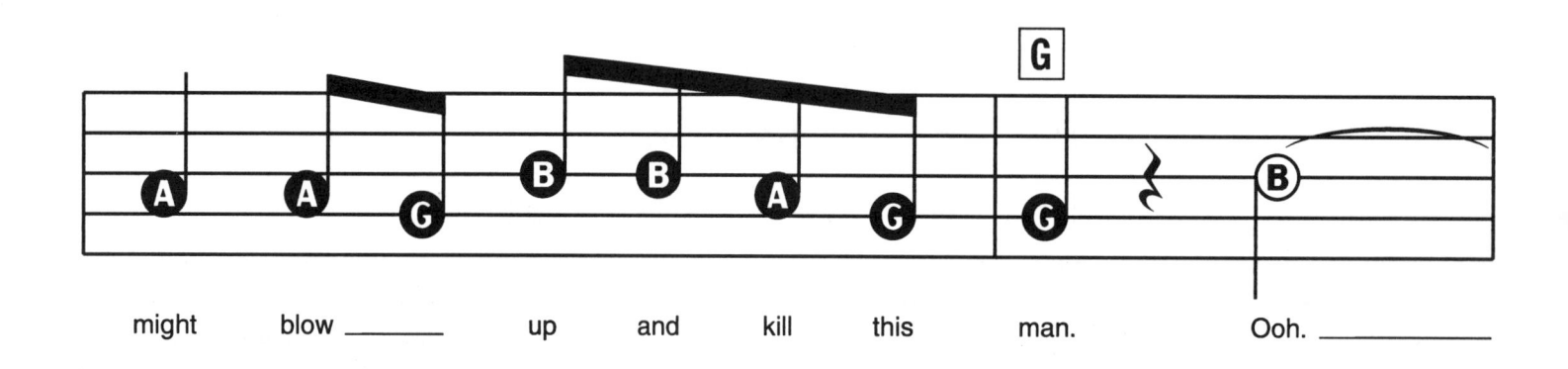

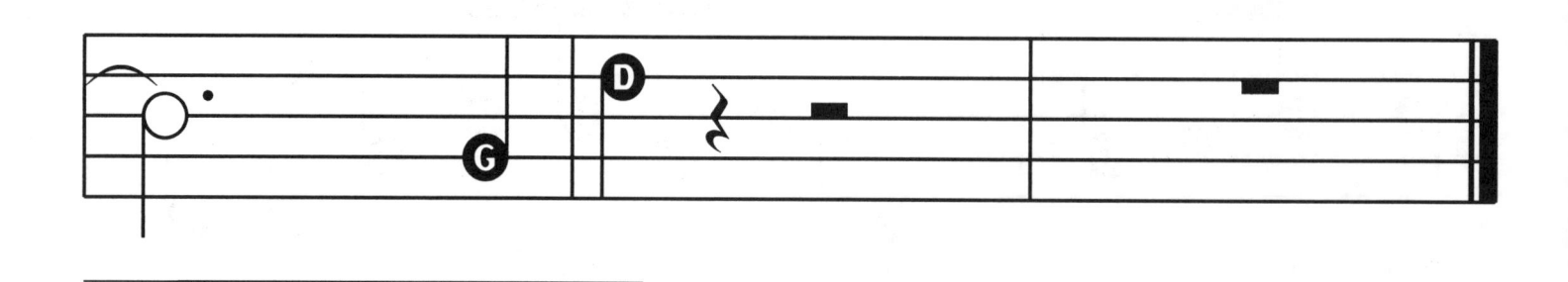

just don't think he'd un - der - stand. And if you tell my heart, my ach - y break - y heart, ____ he might blow _____ up and kill this man. Ooh. ____

Billy The Kid

Registration 7
Rhythm: Country

Words and Music by Billy Dean
and Paul Wilson

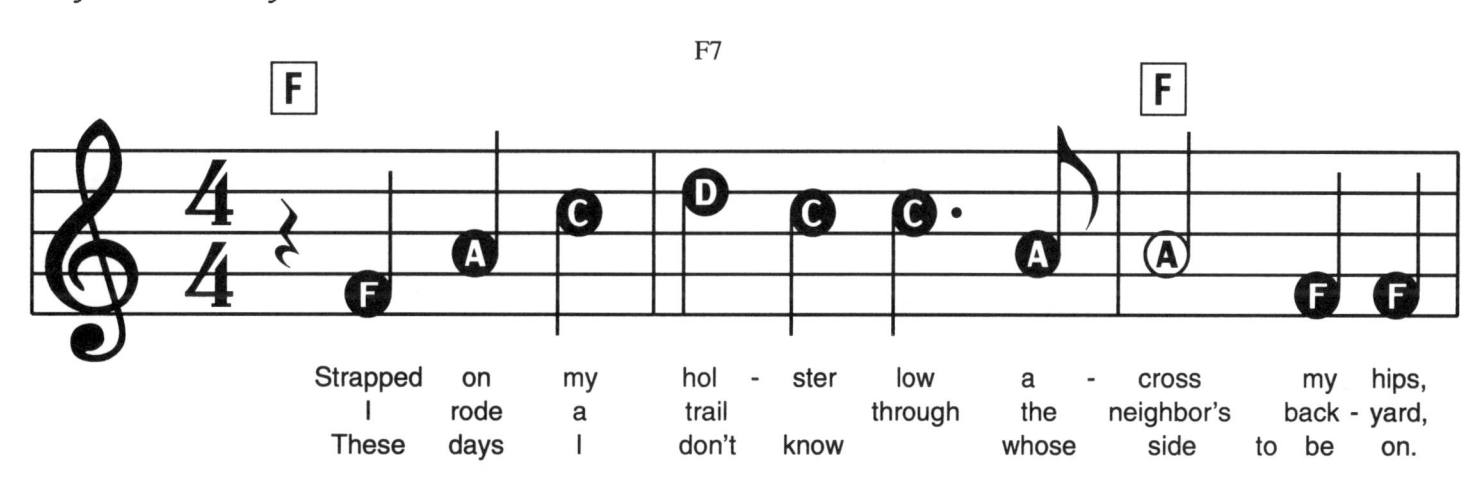

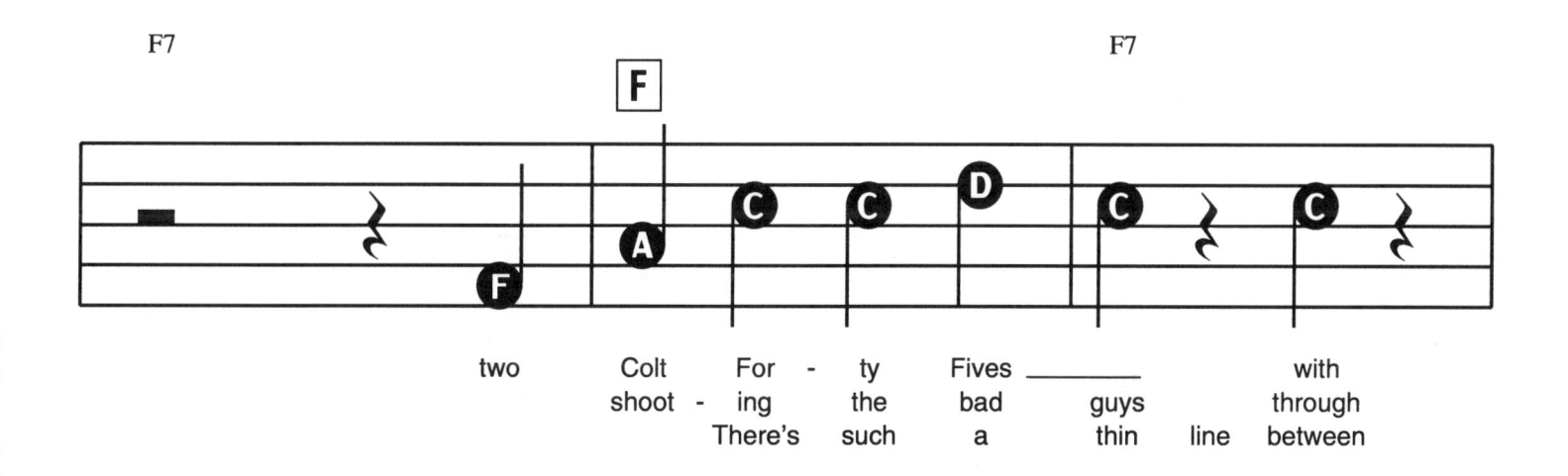

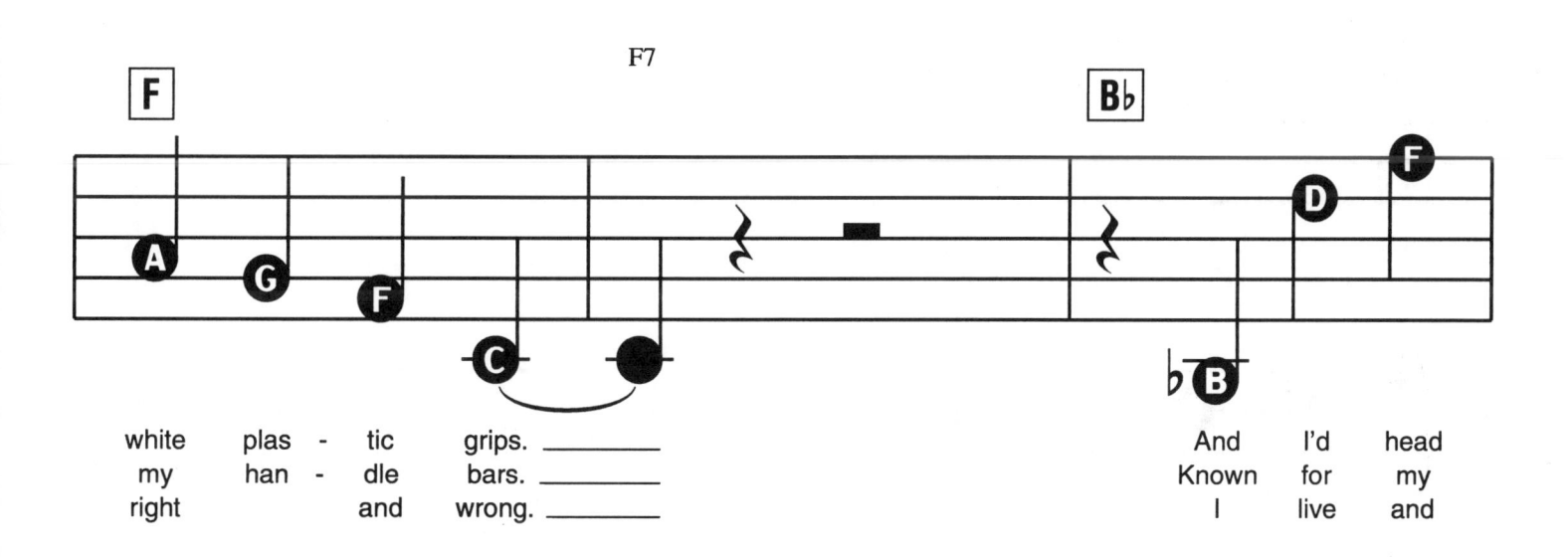

Strapped on my hol - ster low a - cross my hips,
I rode a trail through the neigh - bor's back - yard,
These days I don't know whose side to be on.

two Colt For - ty Fives _____ with
shoot - ing the bad guys with
There's such a thin line between

white plas - tic grips. _____ And I'd head
my han - dle bars. _____ Known for my
right and wrong. _____ I live and

© 1991 EMI BLACKWOOD MUSIC INC. and GREAT CUMBERLAND MUSIC
All Rights Reserved International Copyright Secured Used by Permission

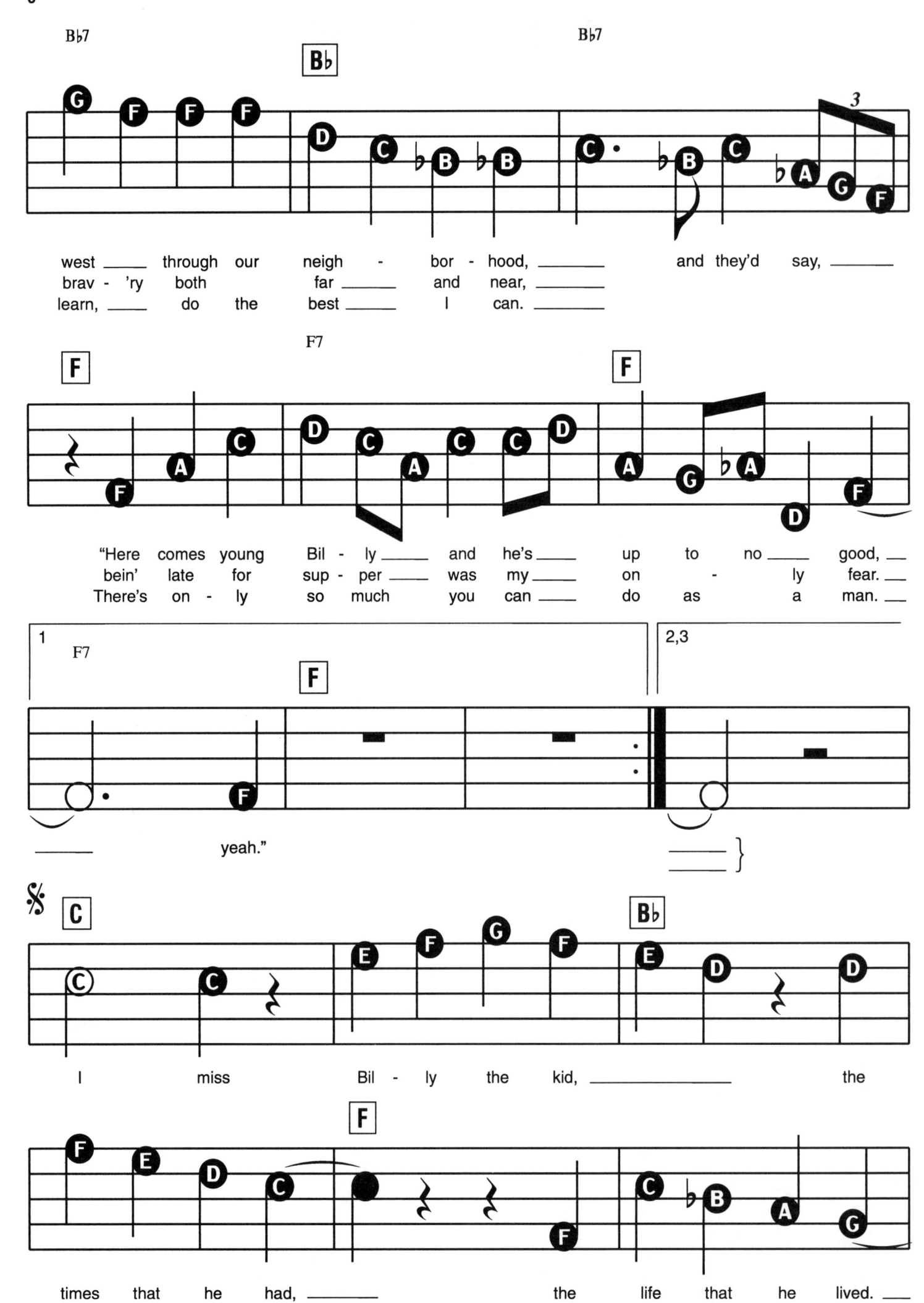

west ____ through our neigh - bor - hood, _____ and they'd say, _____
brav - 'ry both far ____ and near, _____
learn, ____ do the best ____ I can. _____

"Here comes young Bil - ly ____ and he's ____ up to no ____ good, ____
bein' late for sup - per ____ was my ____ on - ly fear. ____
There's on - ly so much you can ____ do as a man. ____

____ yeah."

I miss Bil - ly the kid, _____ the times that he had, _____ the life that he lived. ____

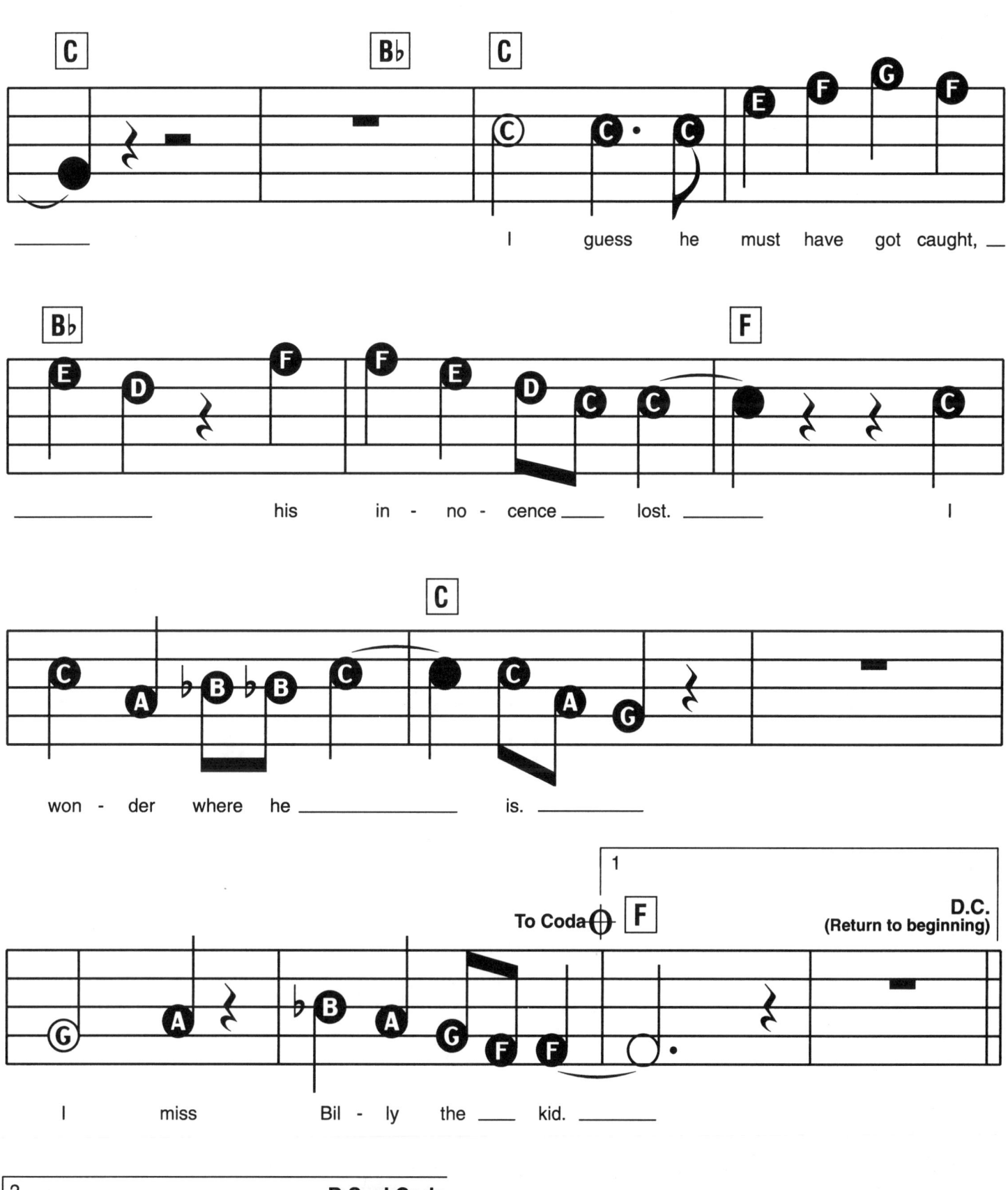

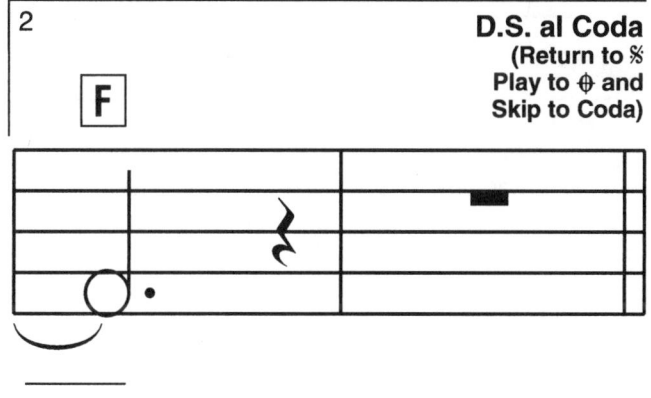

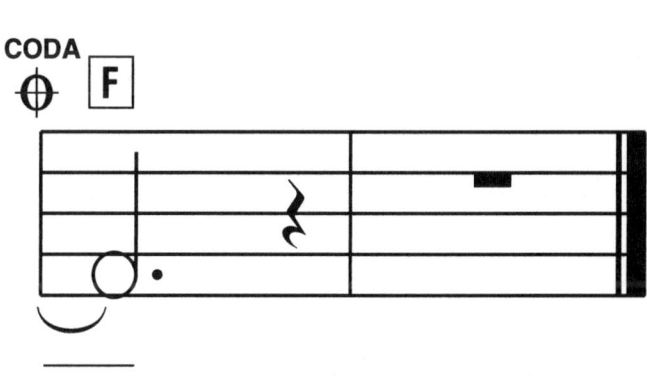

I guess he must have got caught, his in-no-cence lost. I won-der where he is. I miss Bil-ly the kid.

Boot Scootin' Boogie

Registration 2
Rhythm: Swing or Country Shuffle

Words and Music by
Ronnie Dunn

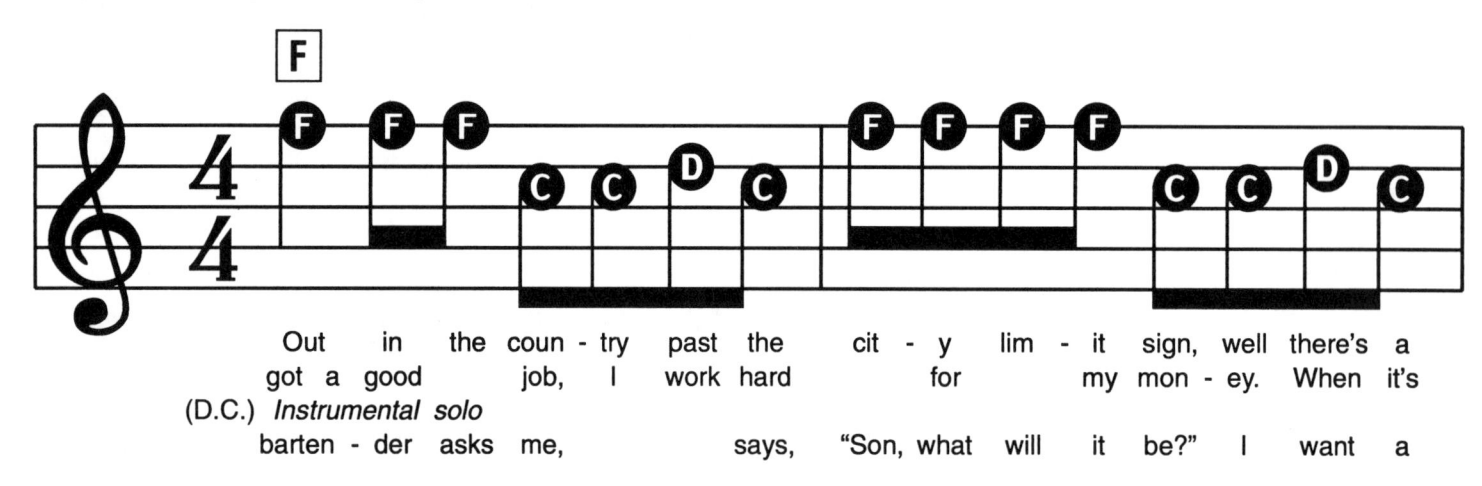

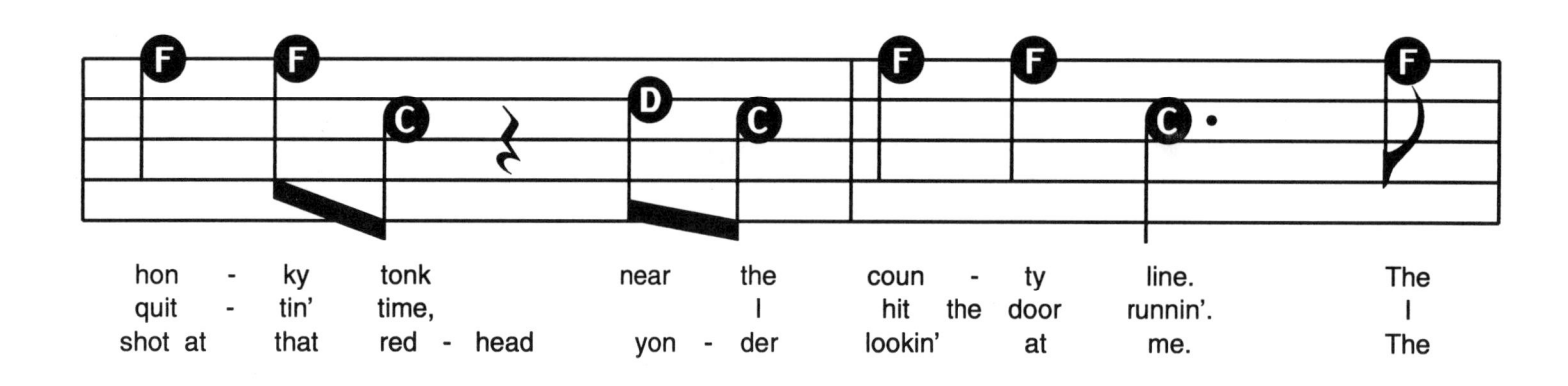

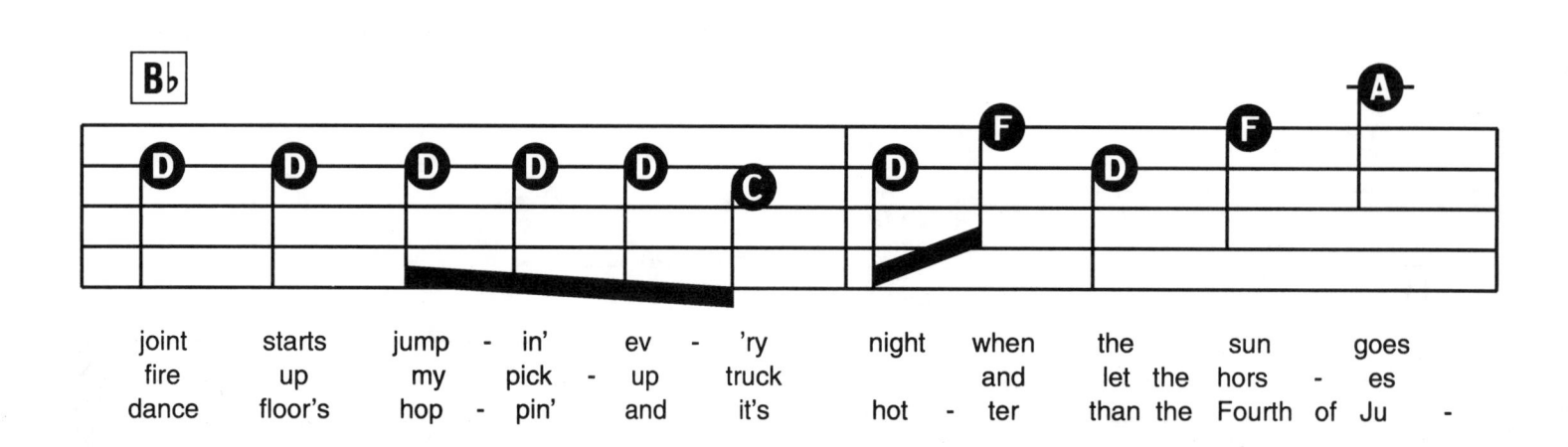

Out in the coun - try past the cit - y lim - it sign, well there's a
got a good job, I work hard for my mon - ey. When it's
(D.C.) *Instrumental solo*
barten - der asks me, says, "Son, what will it be?" I want a

hon - ky tonk near the coun - ty line. The
quit - tin' time, I hit the door runnin'. I
shot at that red - head yon - der lookin' at me. The

joint starts jump - in' ev - 'ry night when the sun goes
fire up my pick - up truck and let the hors - es
dance floor's hop - pin' and it's hot - ter than the Fourth of Ju -

Copyright © 1991 Tree Publishing Co., Inc. and Alfred Avenue Music
All Rights on behalf of Tree Publishing Co., Inc. Administered by Sony Music Publishing, 8 Music Square West, Nashville, TN 37203
International Copyright Secured   All Rights Reserved

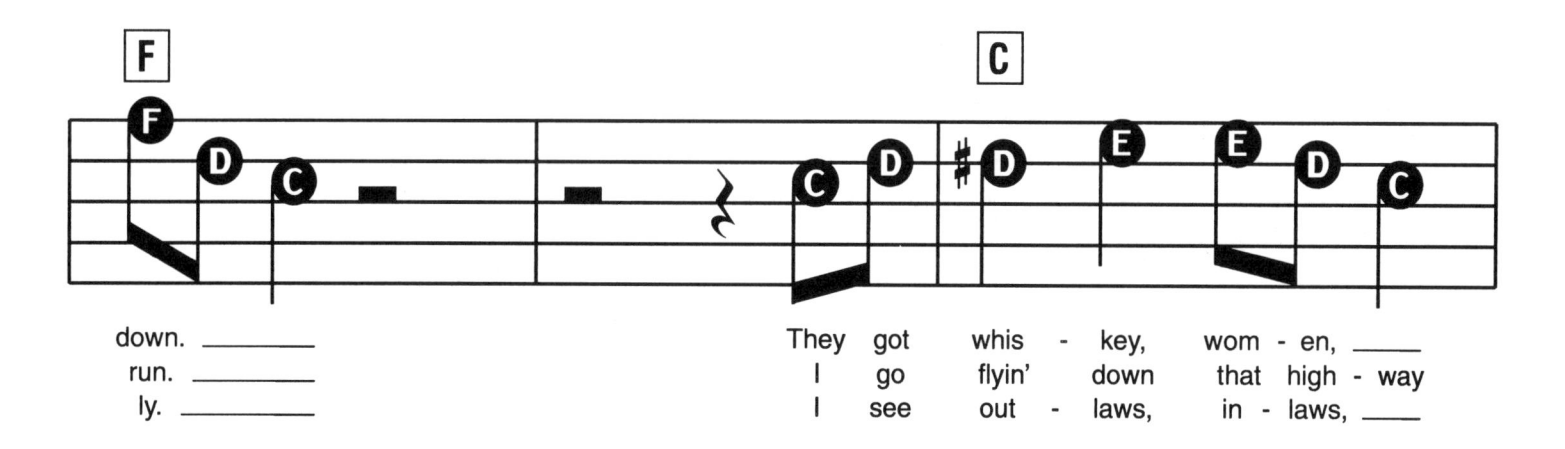

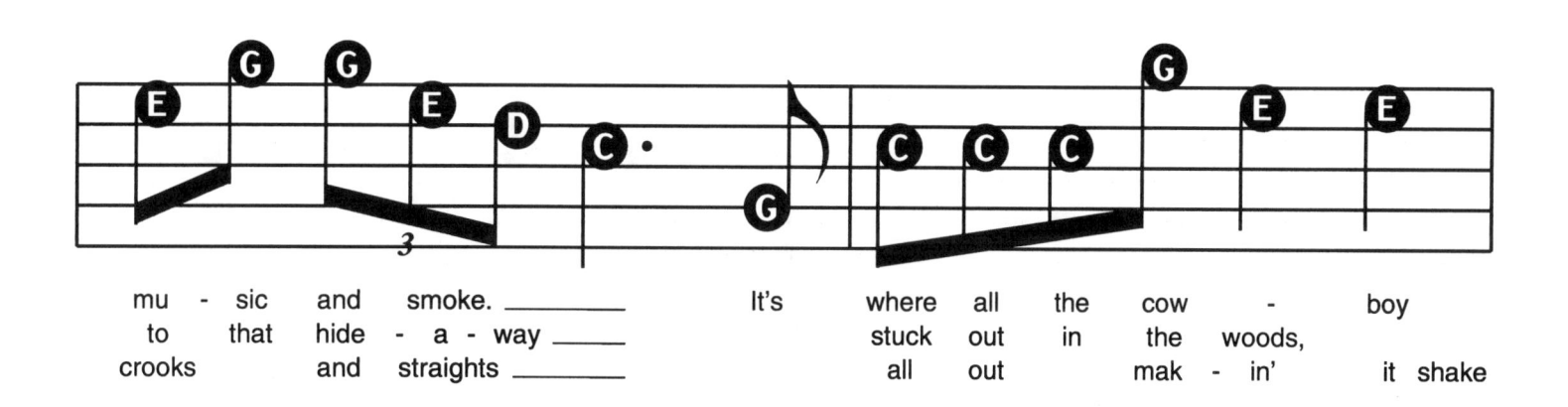

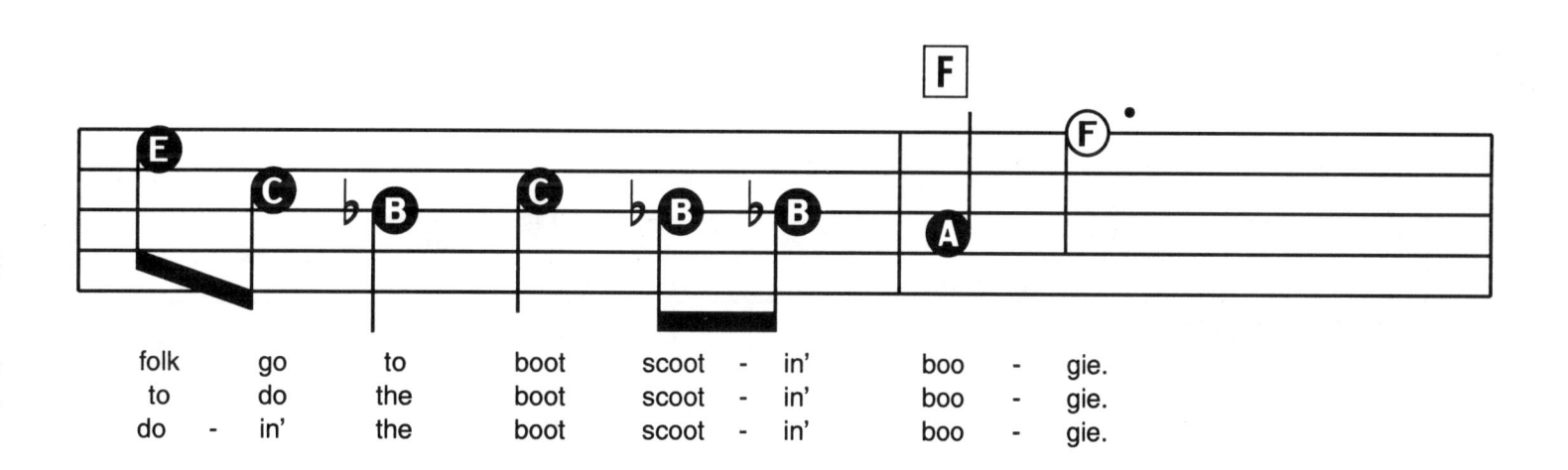

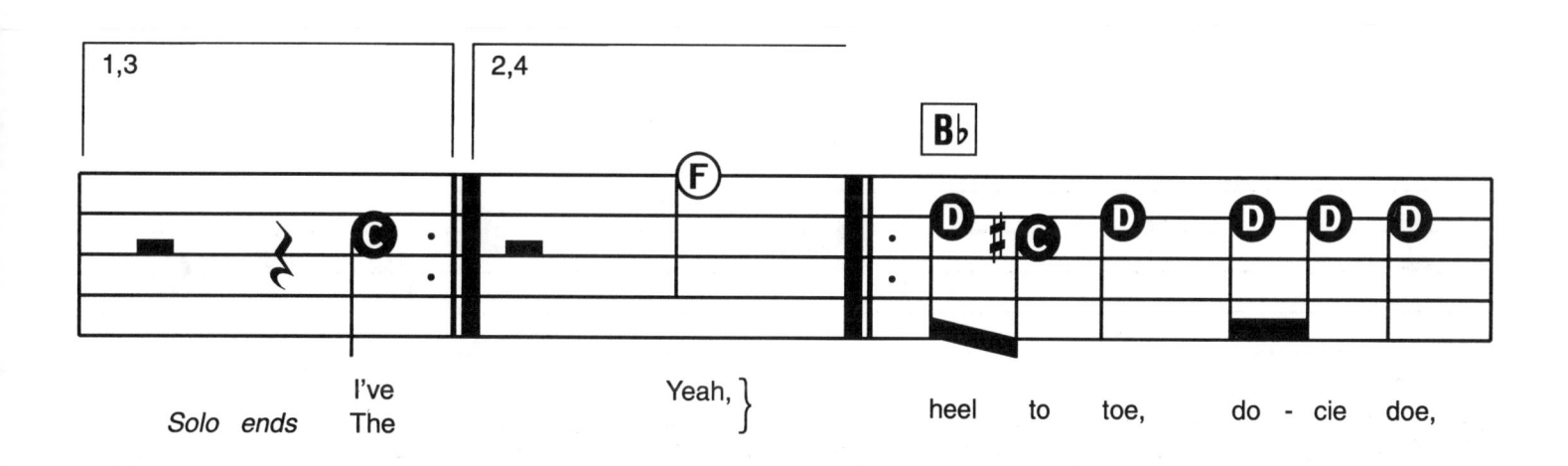

down. / run. / ly.

They got whis-key, wom-en, / I go flyin' down that high-way / I see out-laws, in-laws,

mu-sic and smoke. / to that hide-a-way / crooks and straights

It's where all the cow-boy / stuck out in the woods, / all out mak-in' it shake

folk go to boot scoot-in' boo-gie. / to do the boot scoot-in' boo-gie. / do-in' the boot scoot-in' boo-gie.

1,3 *Solo ends* I've / The

2,4 Yeah, heel to toe, do-cie doe,

come on, ba - by, let's go boot scoot - in'!

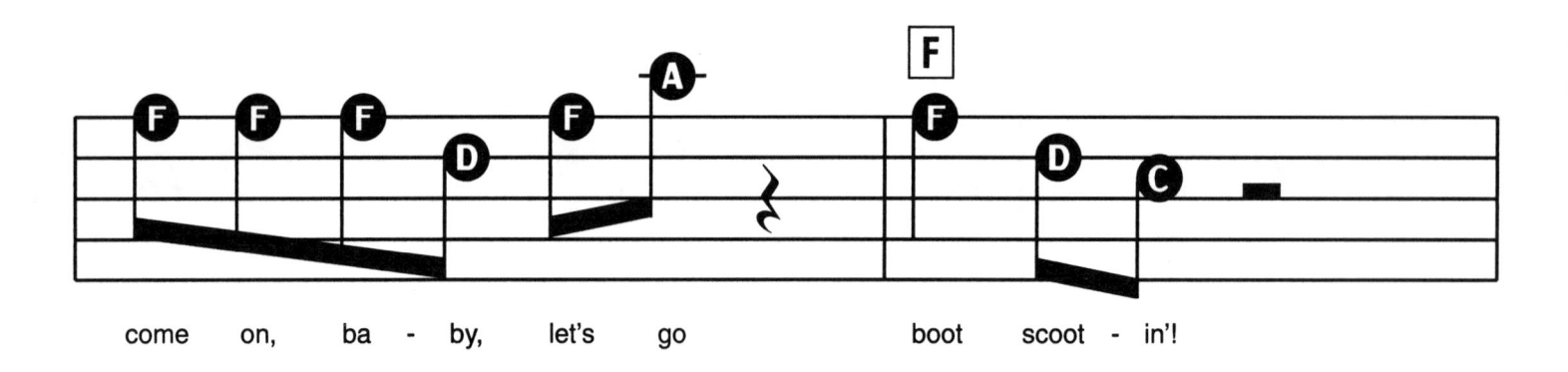

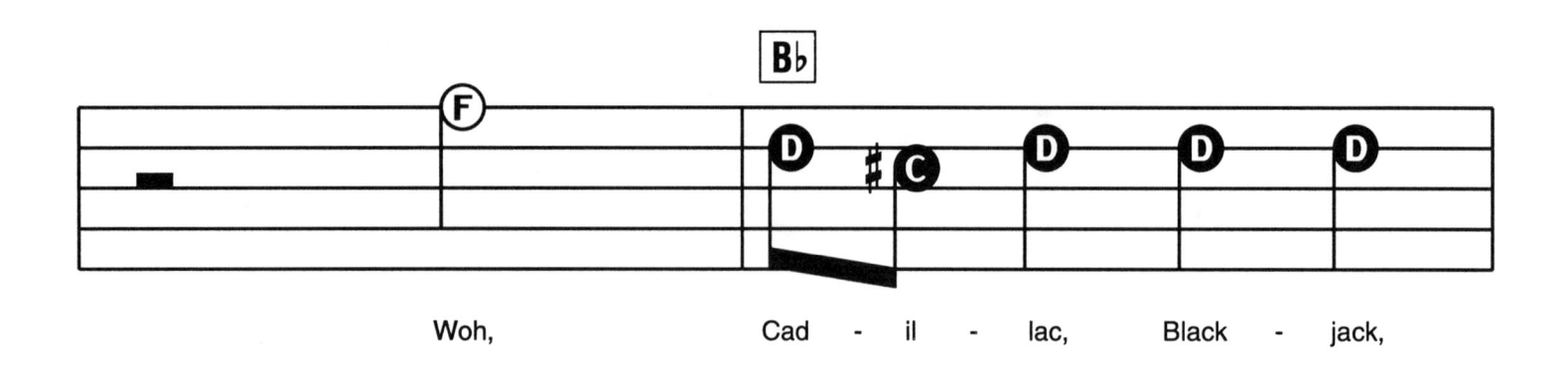

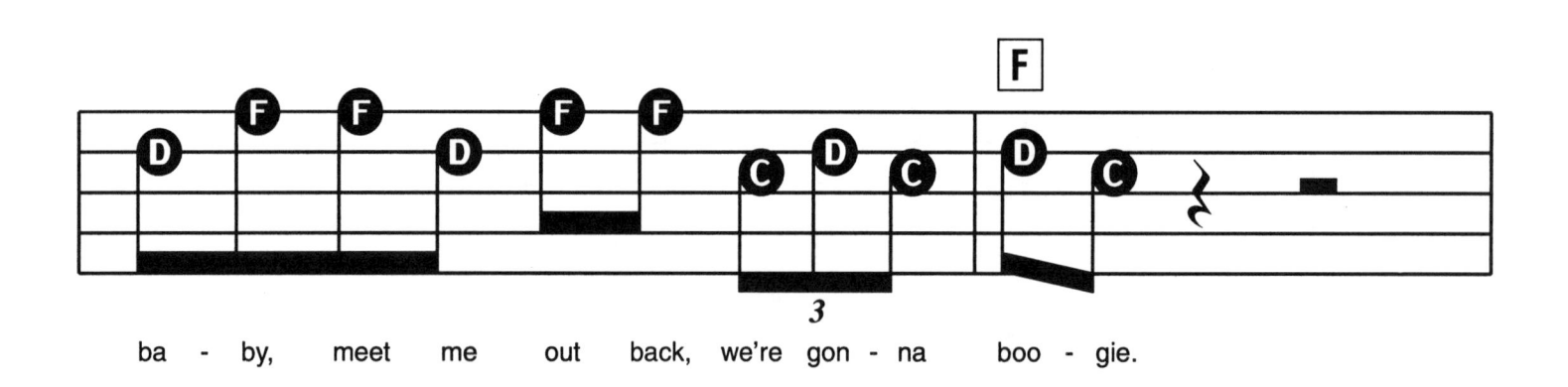

Woh, Cad - il - lac, Black - jack,

ba - by, meet me out back, we're gon - na boo - gie.

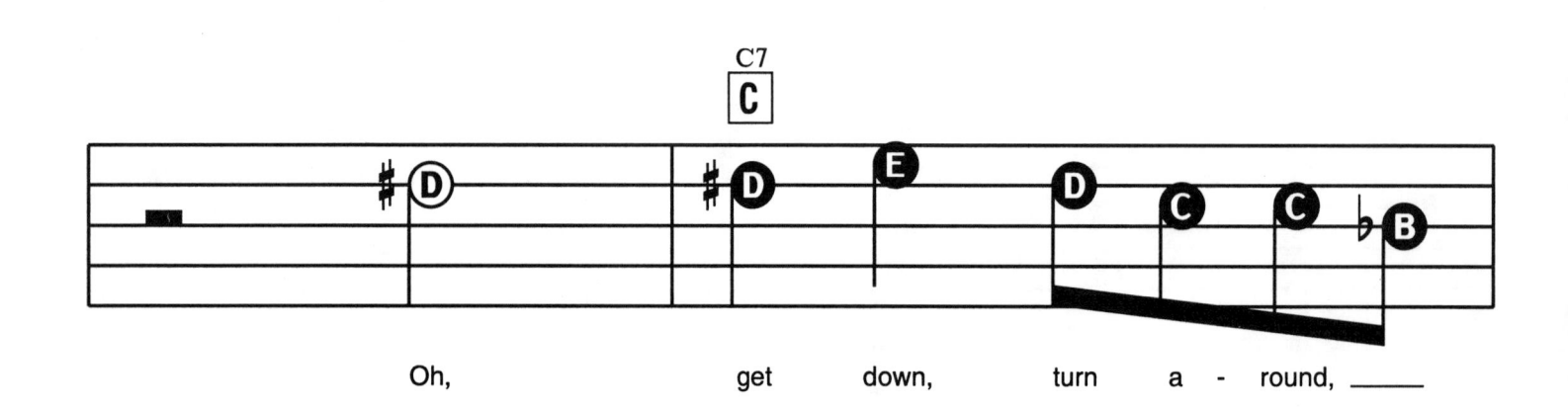

Oh, get down, turn a - round, ___

13

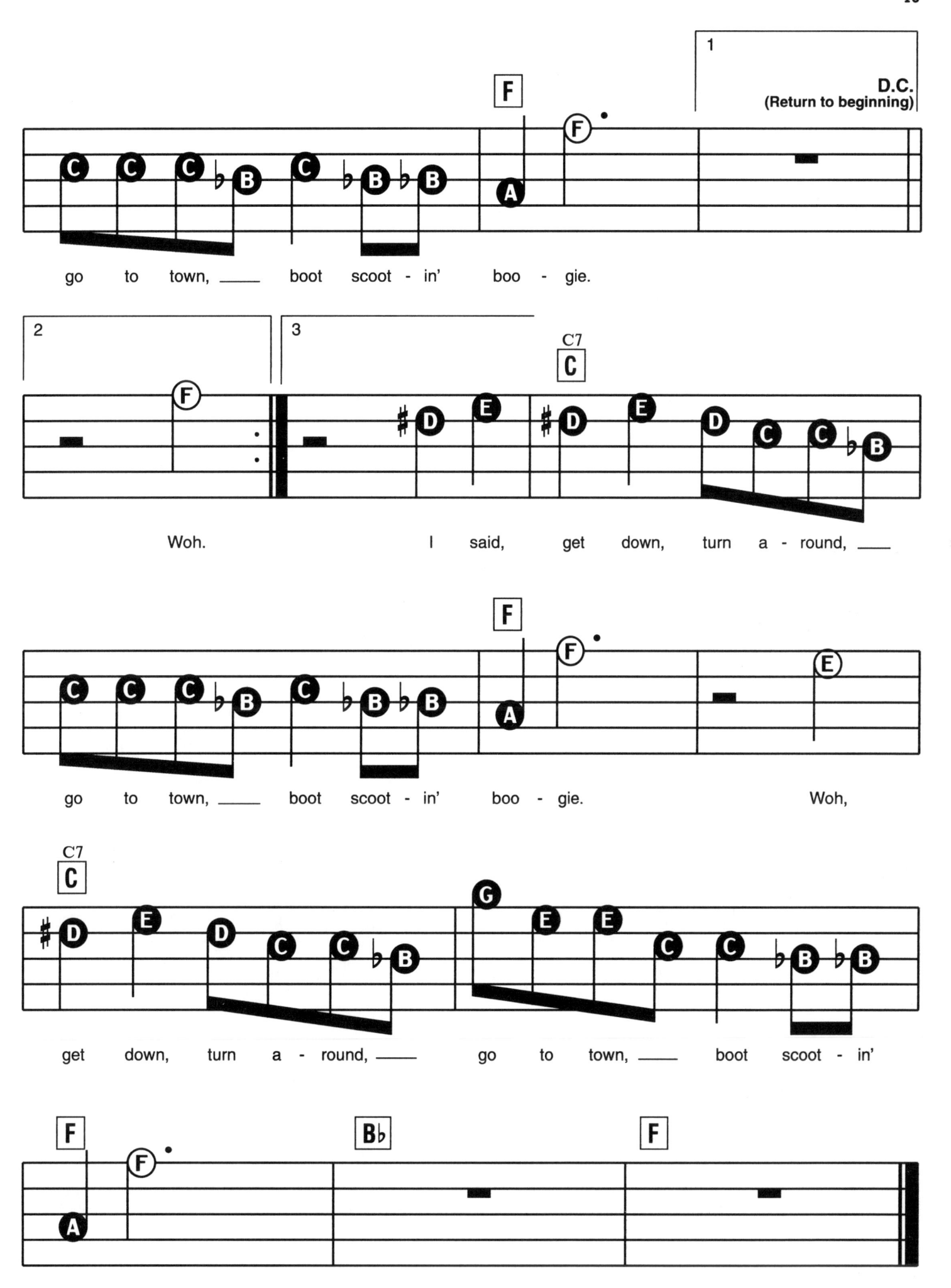

Dallas

Registration 8
Rhythm: Country

Words and Music by Alan Jackson
and Keith Stegall

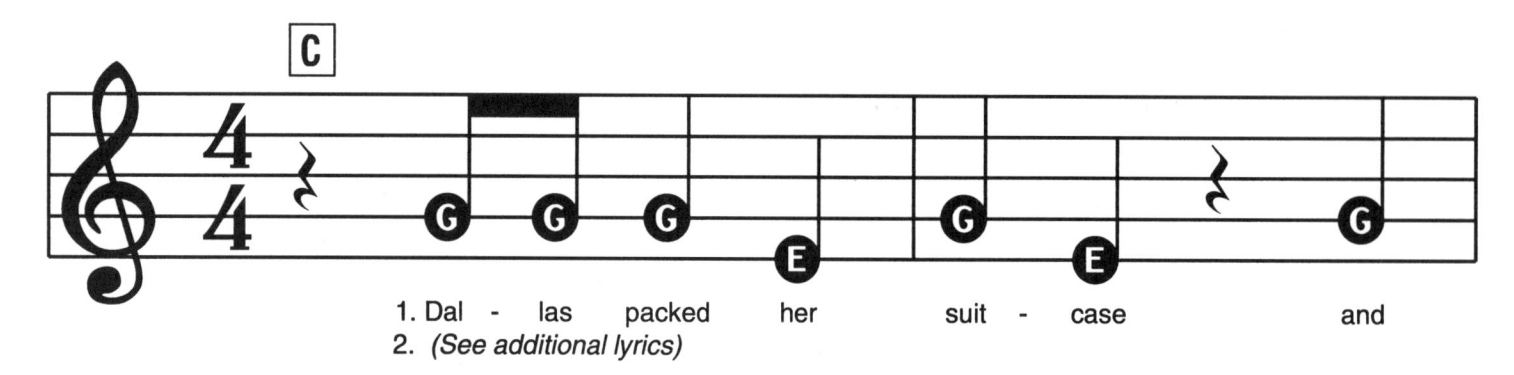

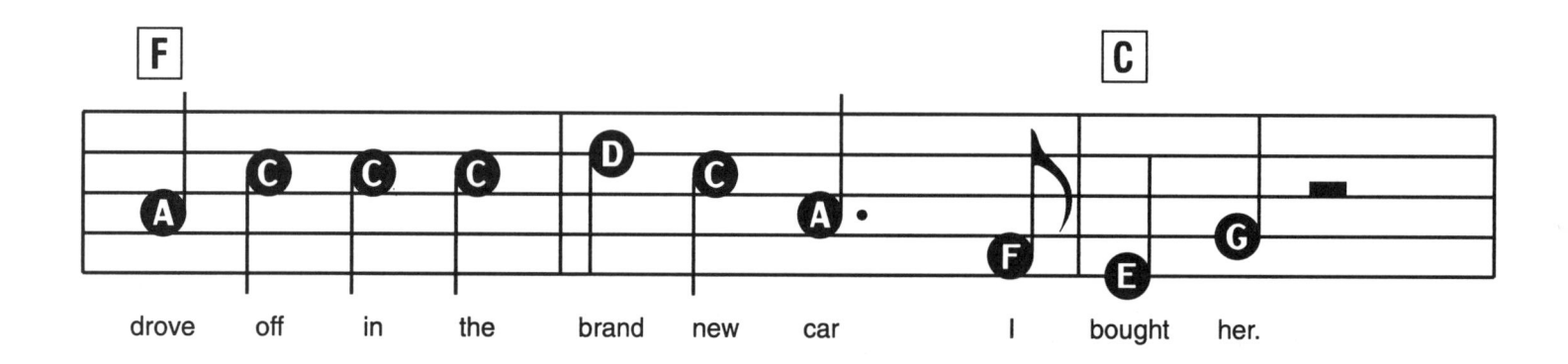

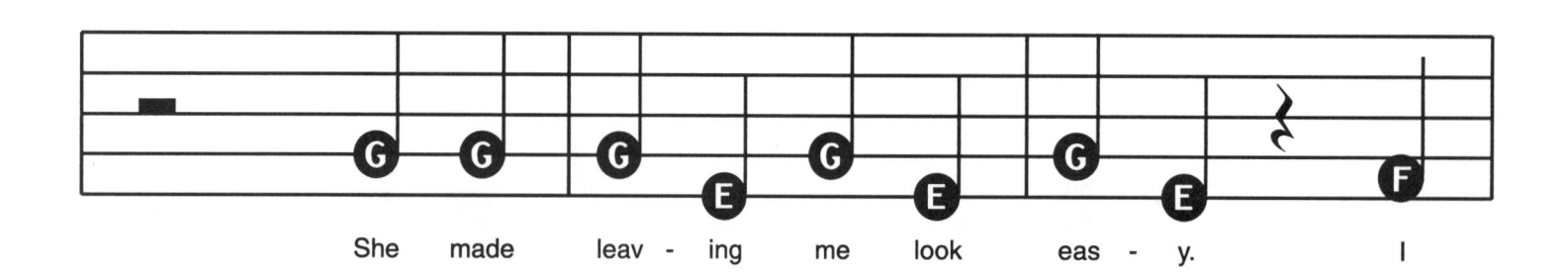

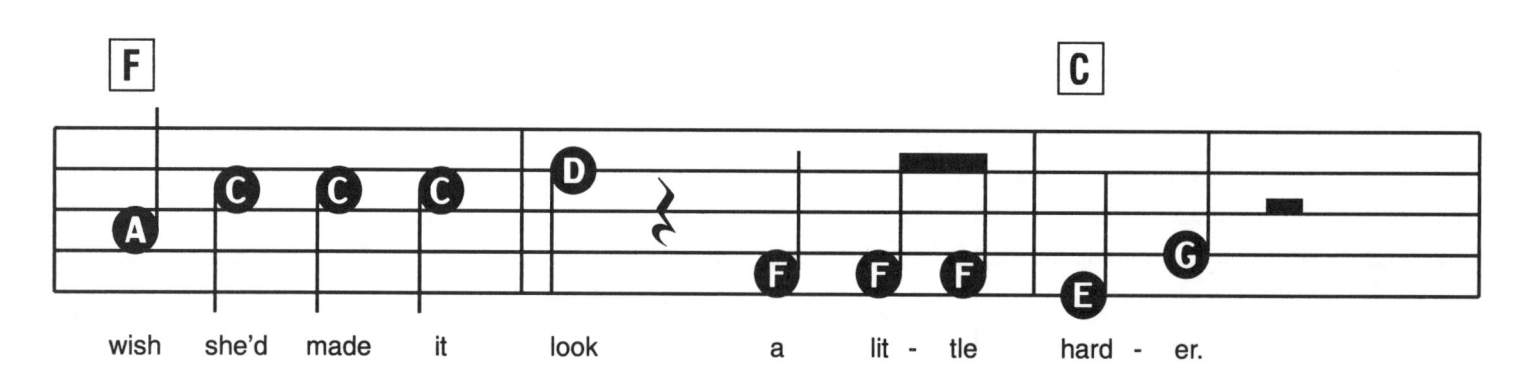

1. Dal - las packed her suit - case and
2. *(See additional lyrics)*

drove off in the brand new car I bought her.

She made leav - ing me look eas - y. I

wish she'd made it look a lit - tle hard - er.

© 1991 WARNER-TAMERLANE PUBLISHING CORP., SEVENTH SON MUSIC and MATTIE RUTH MUSICK
All Rights Reserved

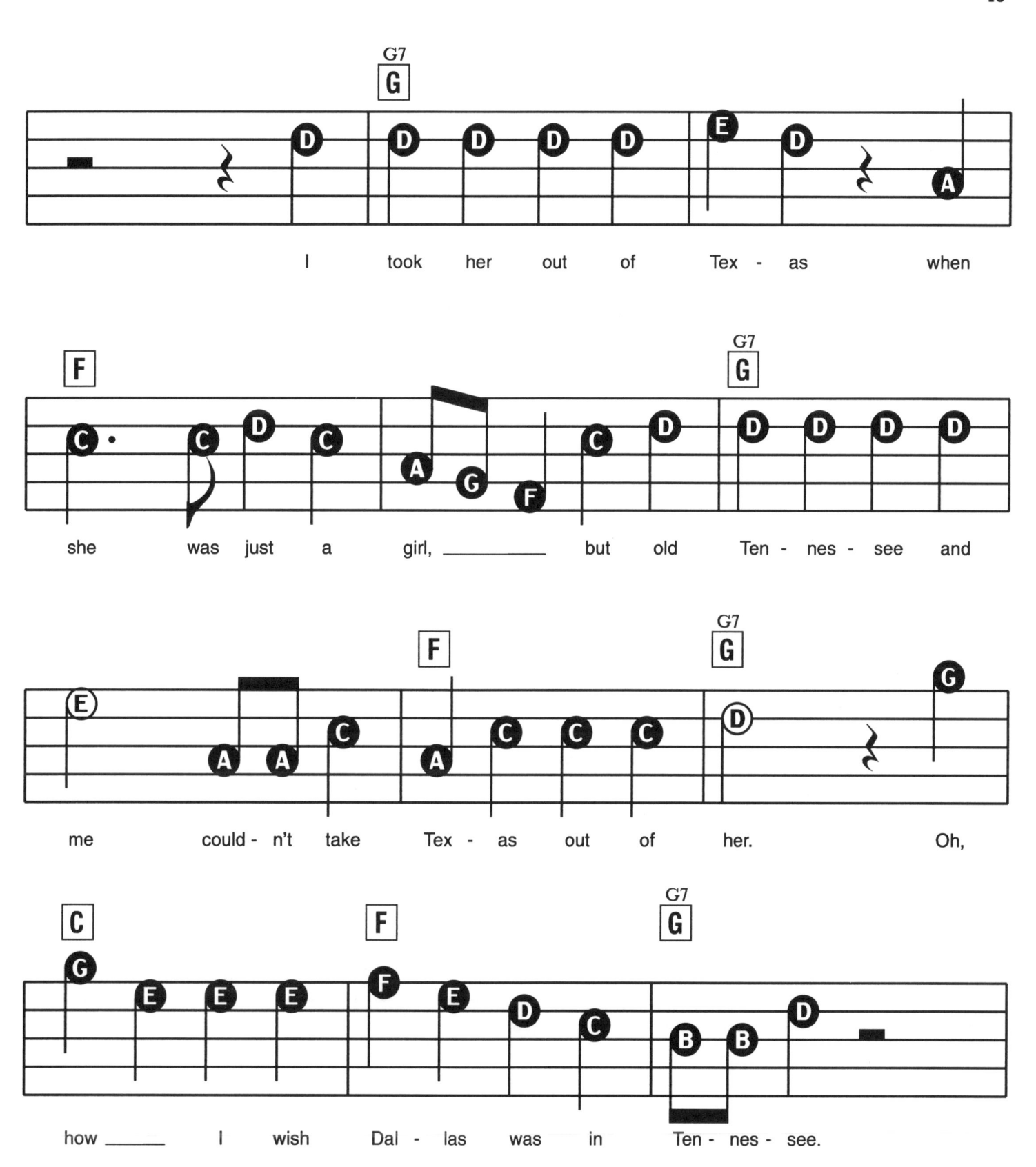

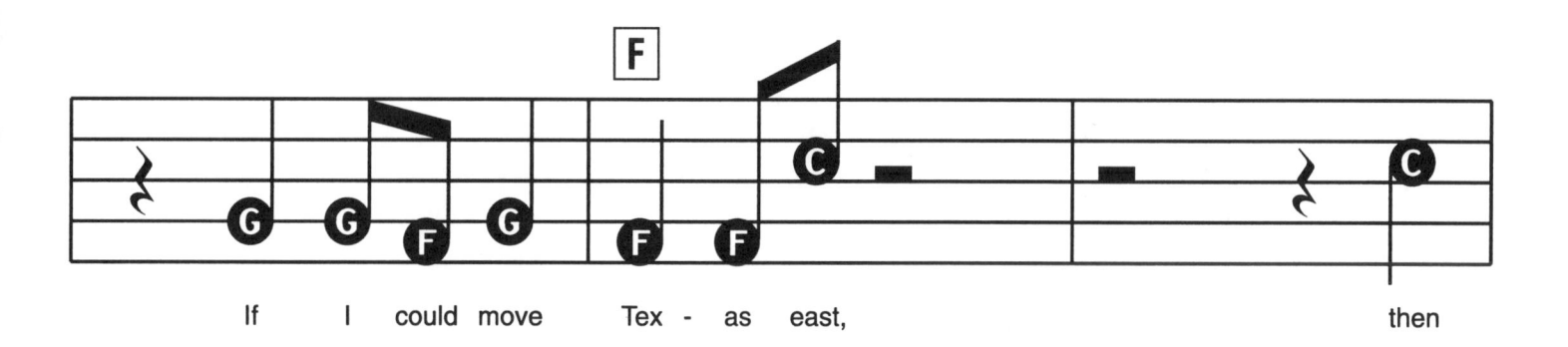

I took her out of Tex - as when she was just a girl, _____ but old Ten - nes - see and me could - n't take Tex - as out of her. Oh, how _____ I wish Dal - las was in Ten - nes - see. If I could move Tex - as east, then she'd be here with me. Then noth - in' else would come be - tween the two of us, if Dal - las was in Ten - nes - see. Dal - las was in Ten - nes - see. Oh, if

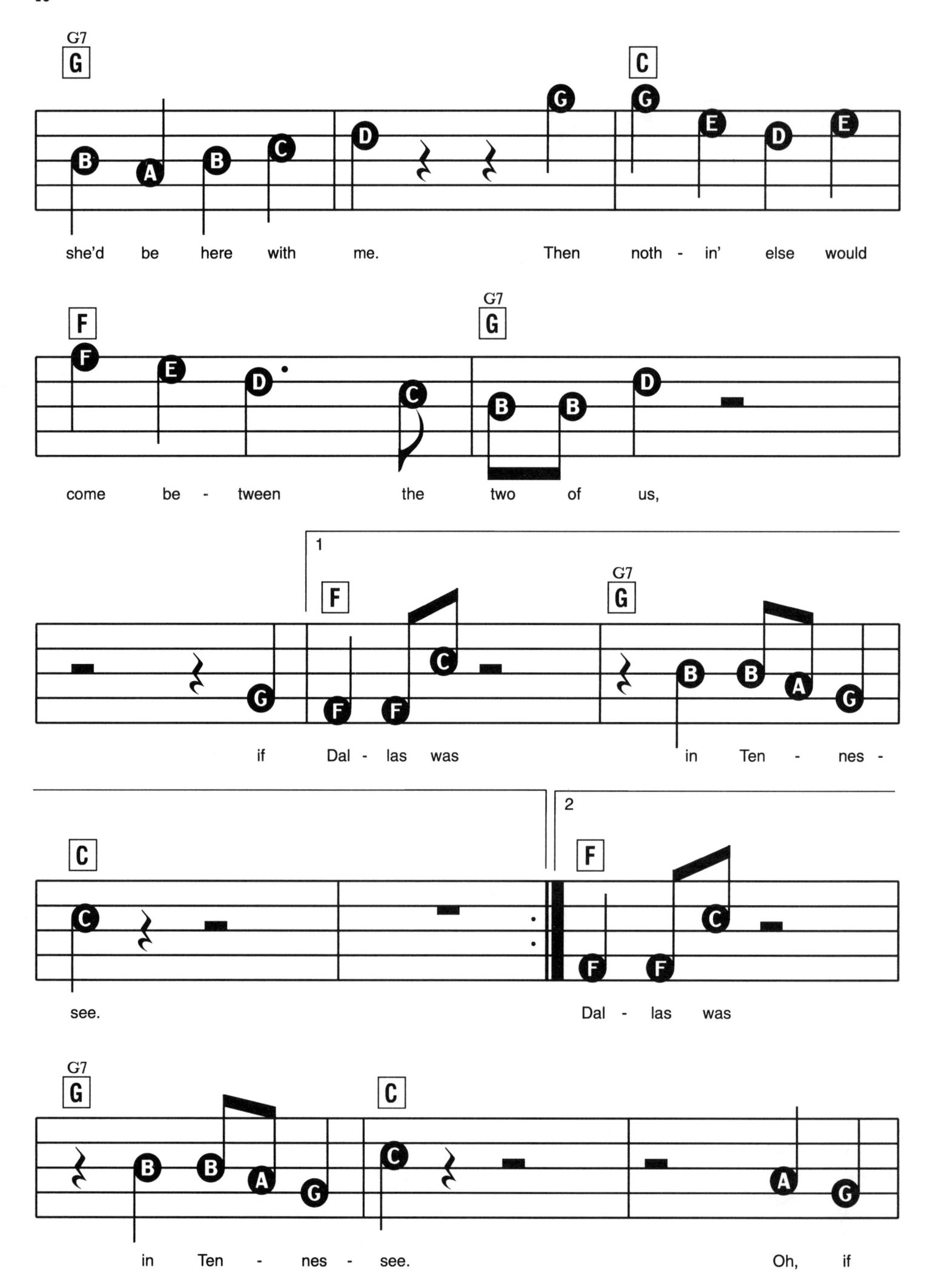

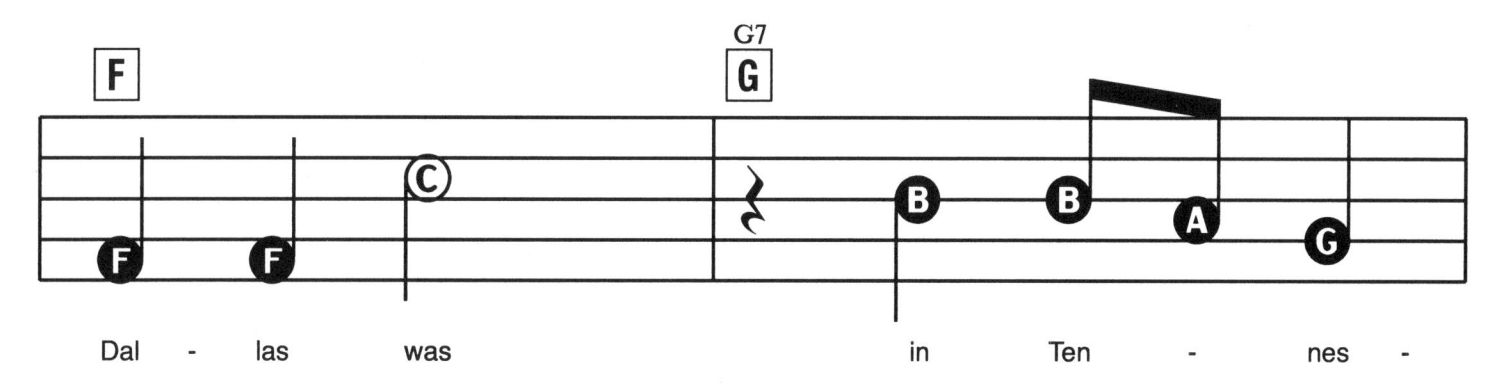

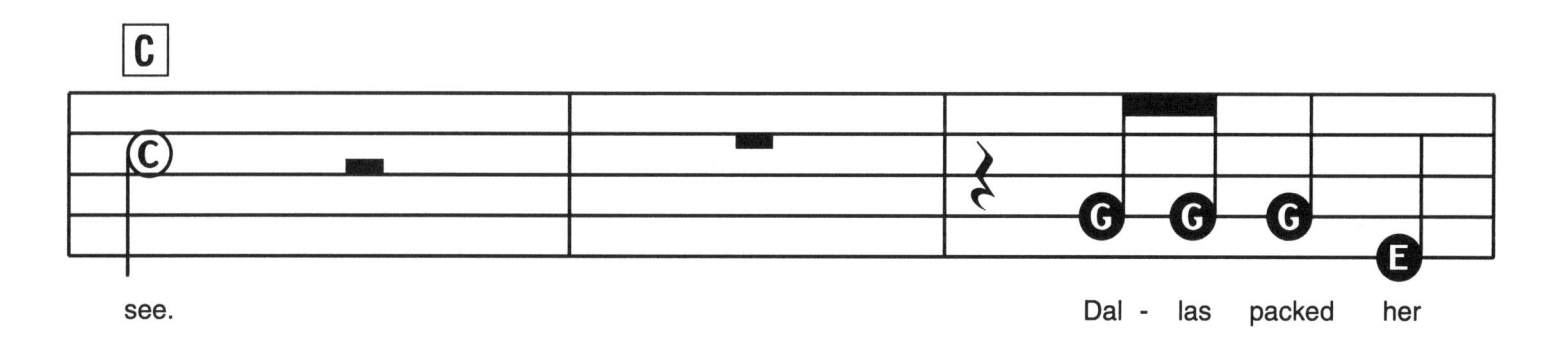

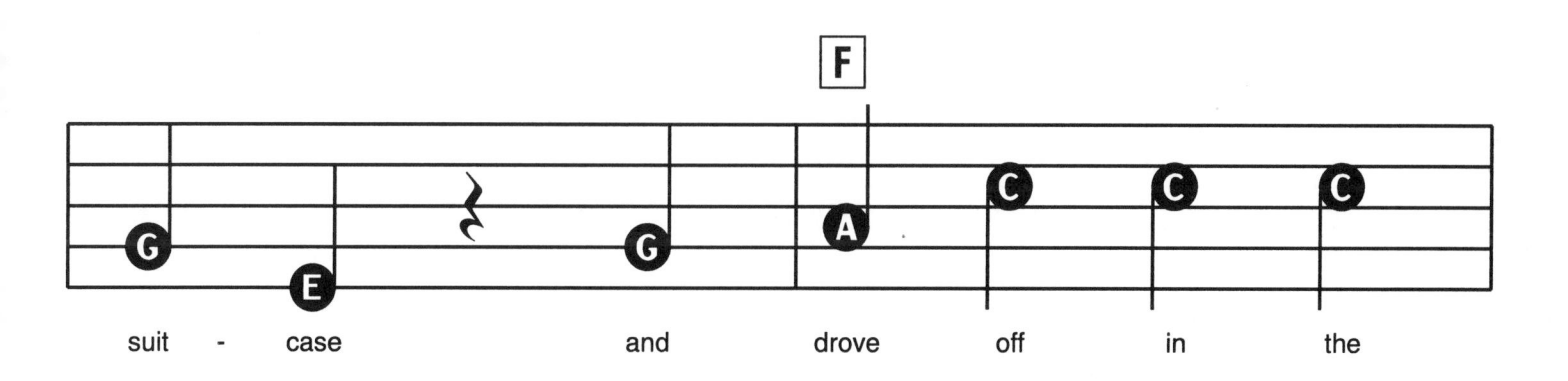

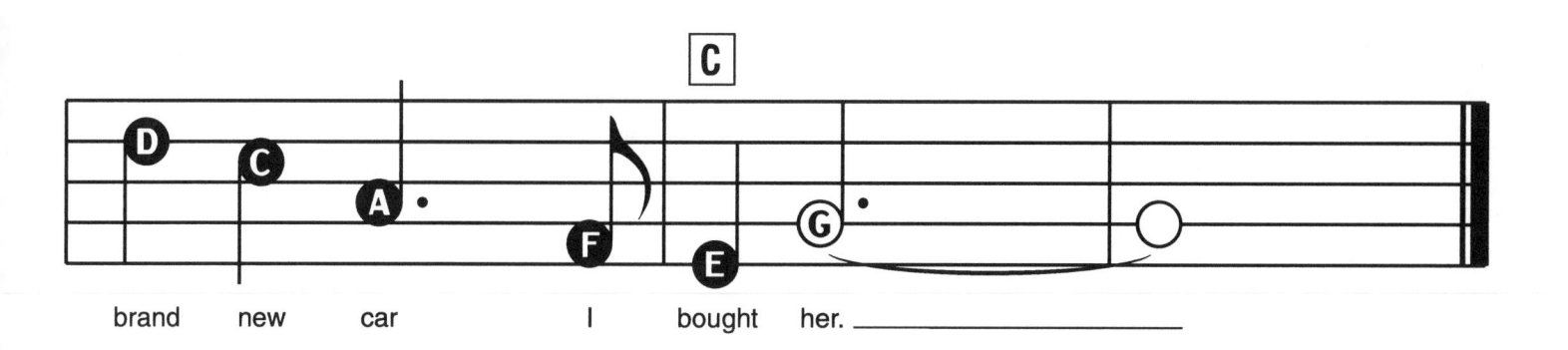

Dal - las was in Ten - nes - see. Dal - las packed her suit - case and drove off in the brand new car I bought her. _____

Additional Lyrics

2. By now she's leaving Memphis
    and everything we had behind her.
  Lord, I hope the gold band on her hand
    will serve as a reminder
  That true love is a treasure
    that's very seldom found.
  But you can't stay together
    if there's no common ground.

Gone As A Girl Can Get

Registration 7
Rhythm: Rock or 8-Beat

Words and Music by
Jerry Max Lane

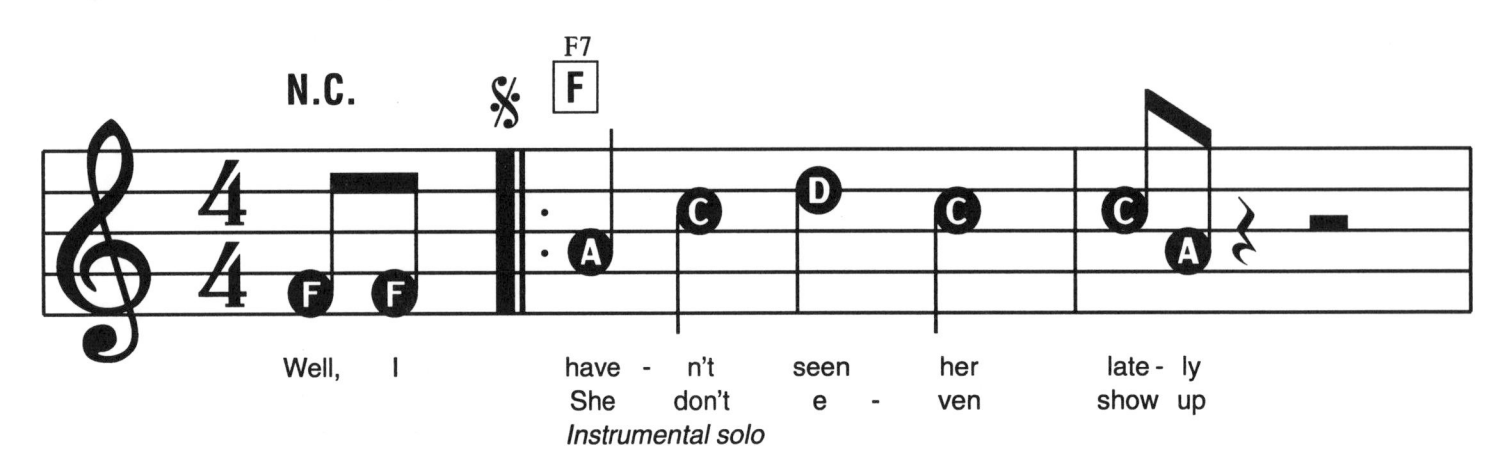

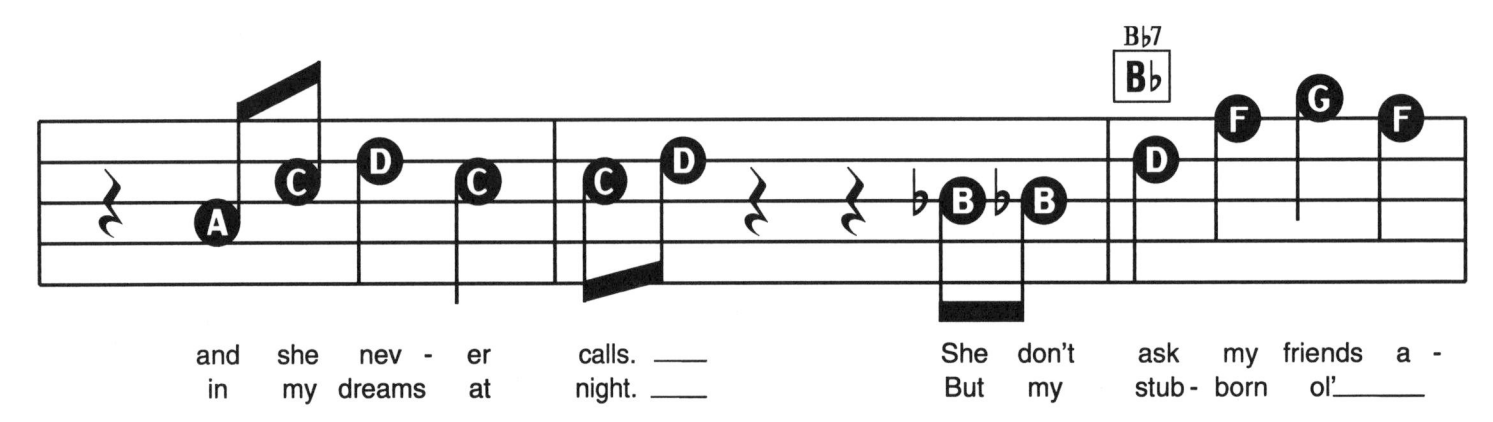

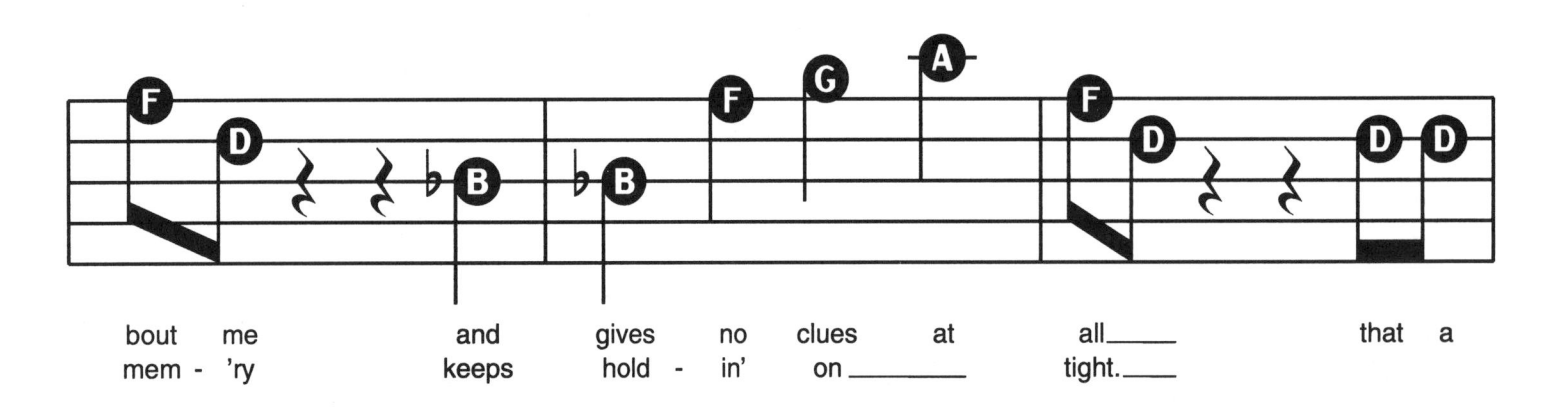

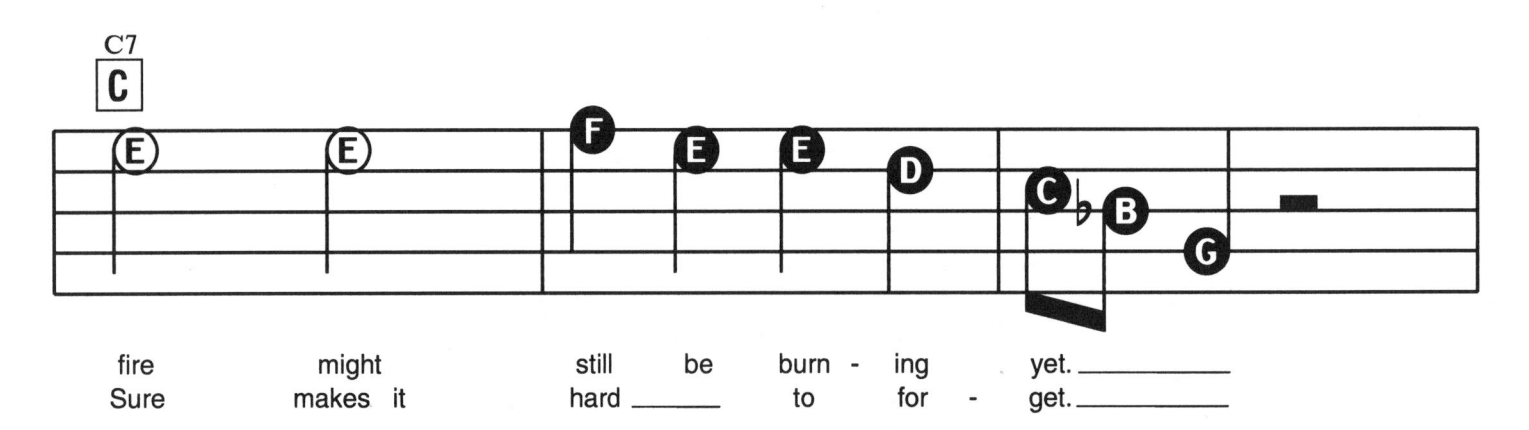

Well, I haven't seen her lately
She don't even show up
Instrumental solo

and she nev-er calls. ___
in my dreams at night. ___
She don't ask my friends a-
But my stub-born ol' ___

bout me and gives no clues at all ___ that a
mem-'ry keeps hold-in' on ___ tight. ___

fire might still be burn-ing yet. ___
Sure makes it hard to for-get. ___

Copyright © 1992 O-Tex Music (BMI) and Jerry Max Music (BMI)
1000 18th Avenue South, Nashville, TN 37212
International Copyright Secured   All Rights Reserved

Well, I'd say she's a - bout as gone as a girl can
She's a - bout as gone as a girl can

1
F7

get.

2,3
F7

get.
Solo ends

B♭7

She's out - ta here, she dis - ap - peared with - out ___ a

A7 **A♭7** **G7**

trace. ___ More or less un - im -

C7

pressed by the tears on my face. ___

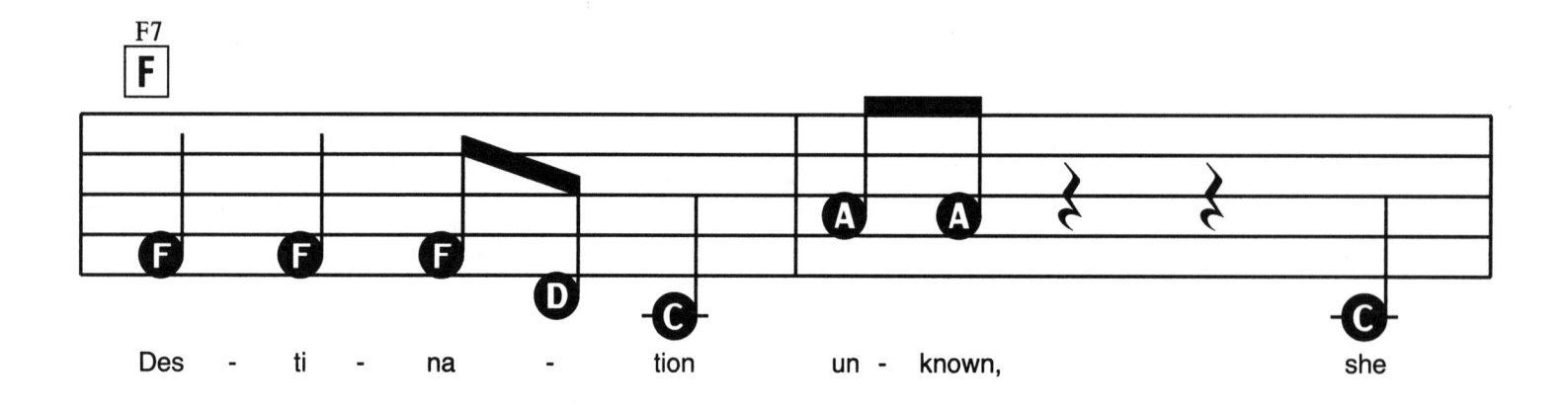

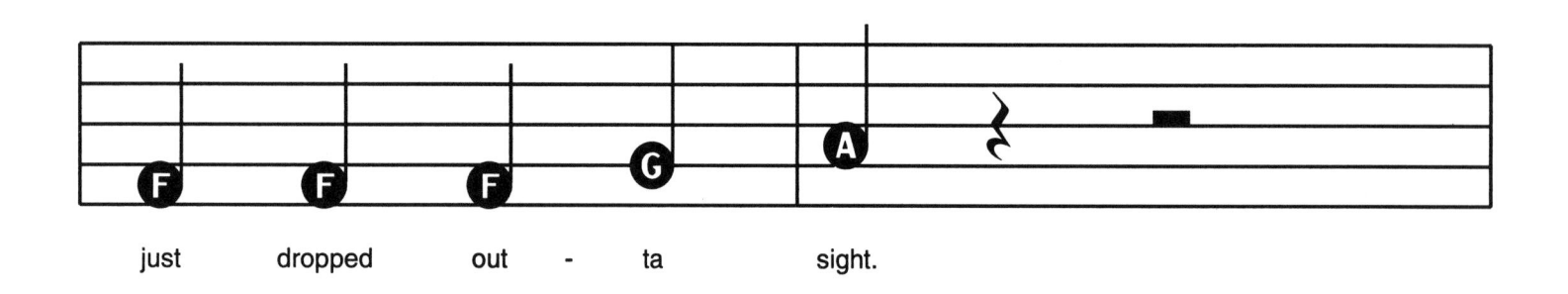

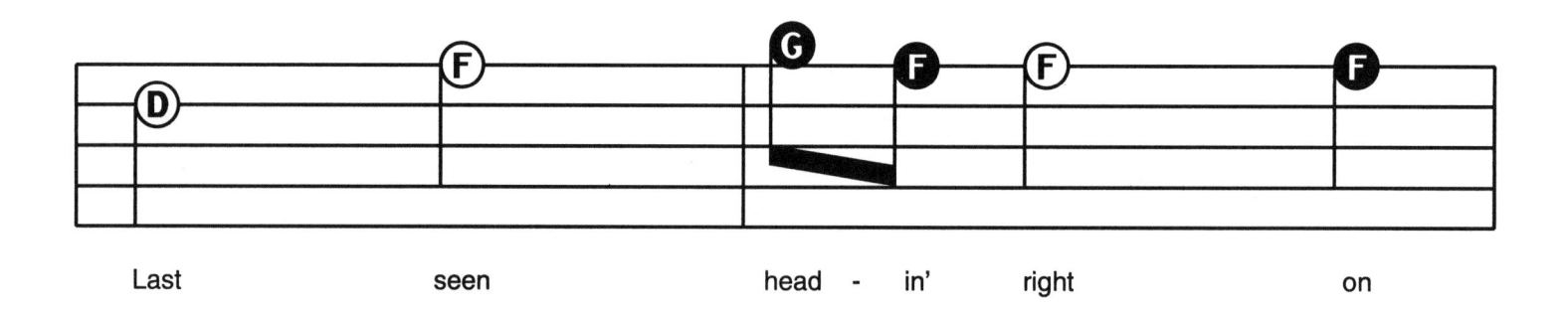

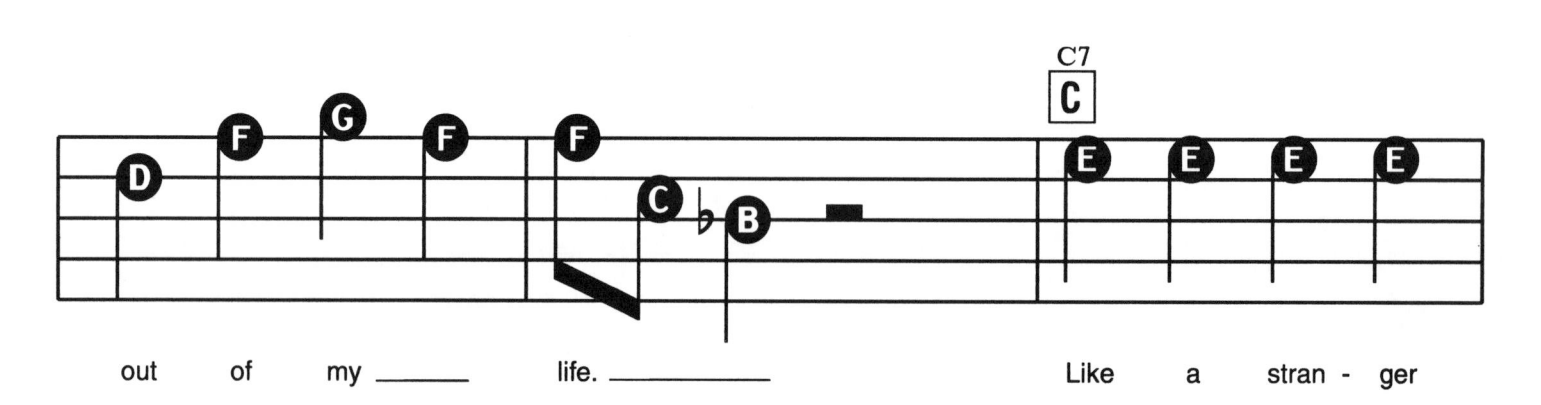

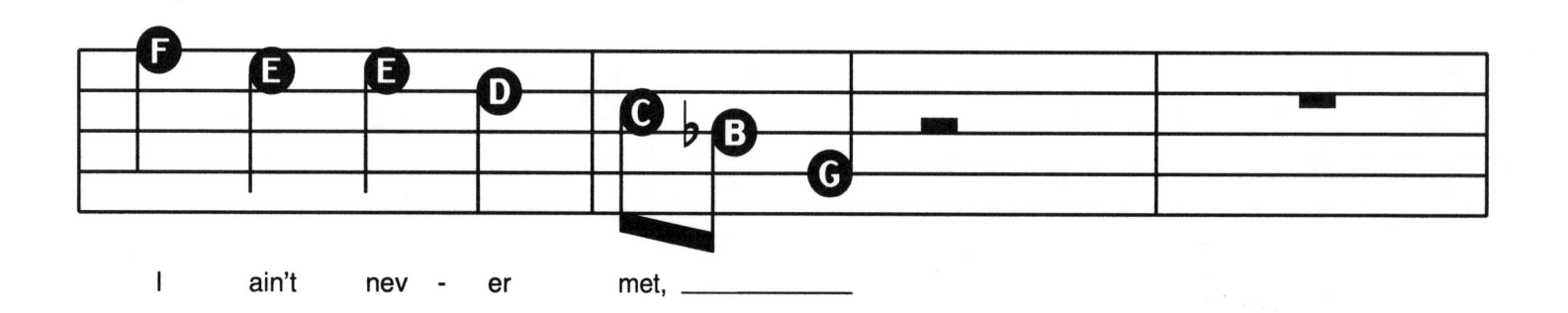

Des - ti - na - tion un - known, she just dropped out - ta sight. Last seen head - in' right on out of my life. Like a stran - ger I ain't nev - er met, she's a - bout as gone as a girl can get.

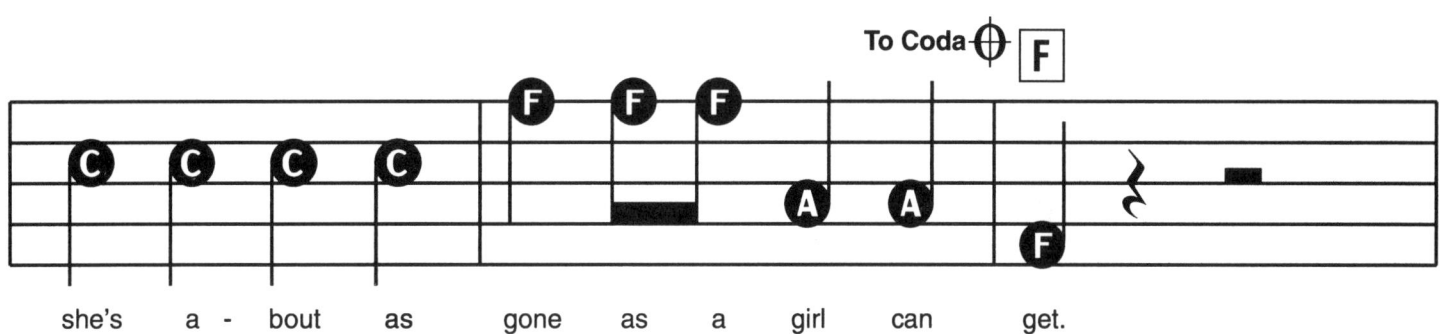

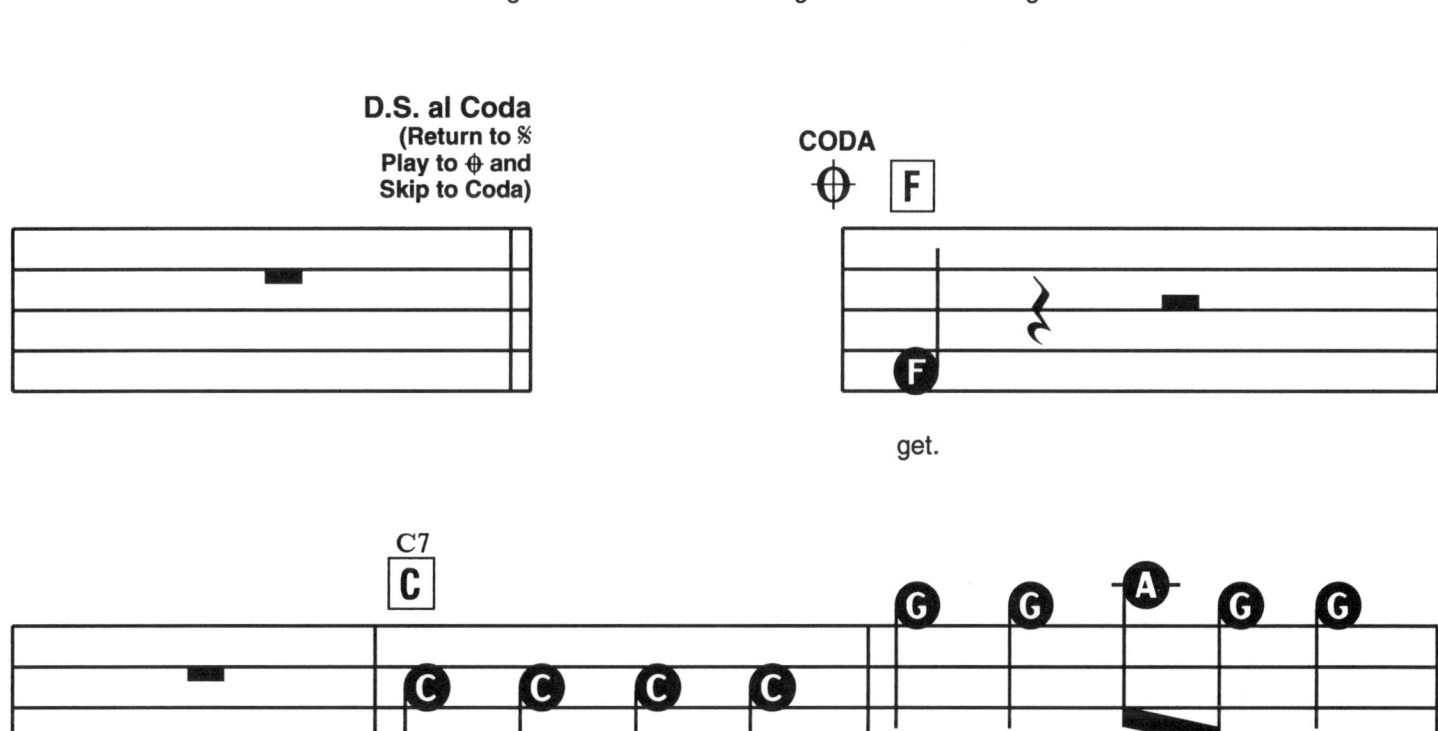

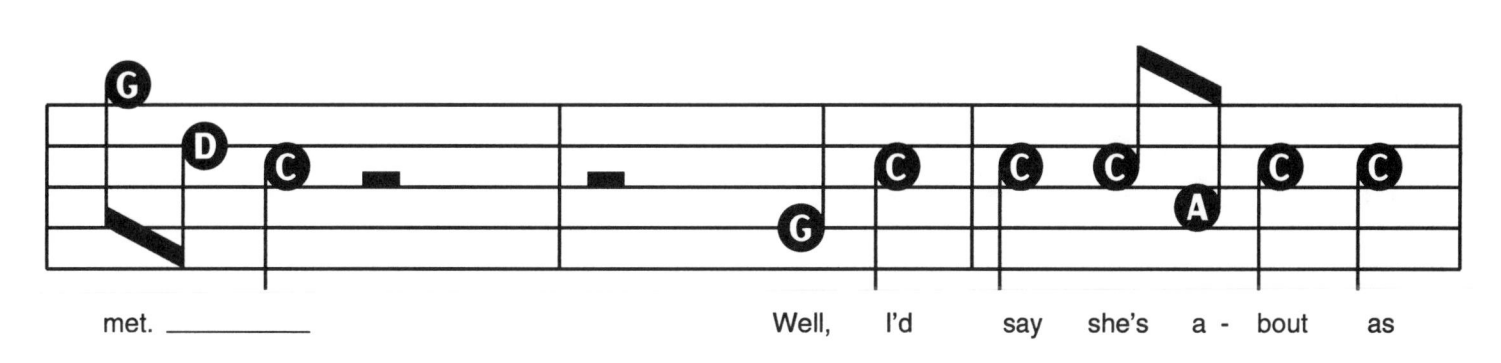

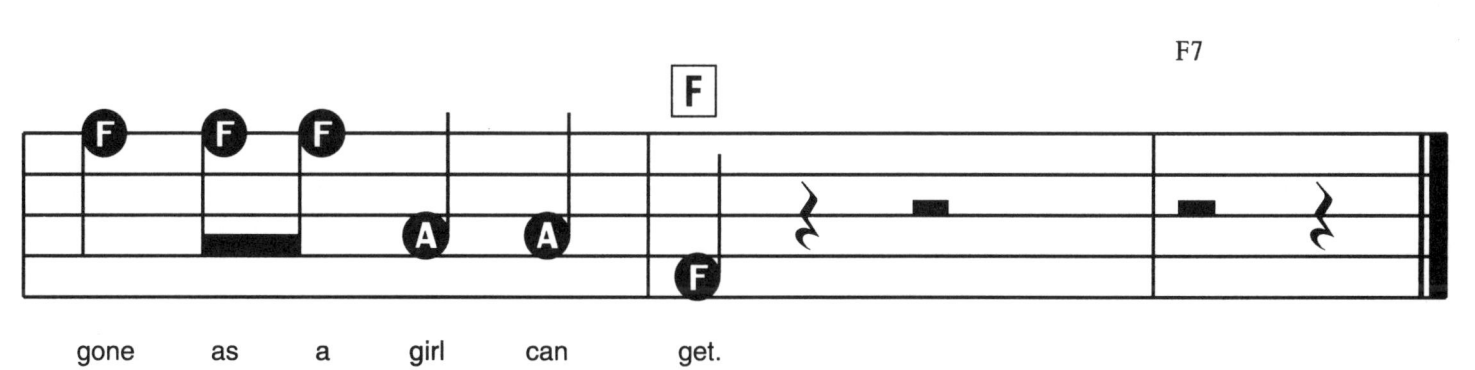

D.S. al Coda
(Return to 𝄋
Play to ⊕ and
Skip to Coda)

CODA

get.

Like a stran - ger I ain't nev - er

met. _____ Well, I'd say she's a - bout as

gone as a girl can get.

I Saw The Light

Registration 9
Rhythm: Country Rock

Words and Music by Lisa Angelle
and Andrew Gold

1. I laid a red rose on your front porch and wrote "I love you," on a note. I rang your doorbell and turned to go.

(D.S.) *Instrumental solo*

cheatin' hands off my red dress 'cause I ain't wearin' this thing for you. I see you clearly now and your lies, too.

Copyright © 1991 Sister Elizabeth Music, administered by Great Eastern Music Co. and Sluggosongs (BMI)
International Copyright Secured All Rights Reserved

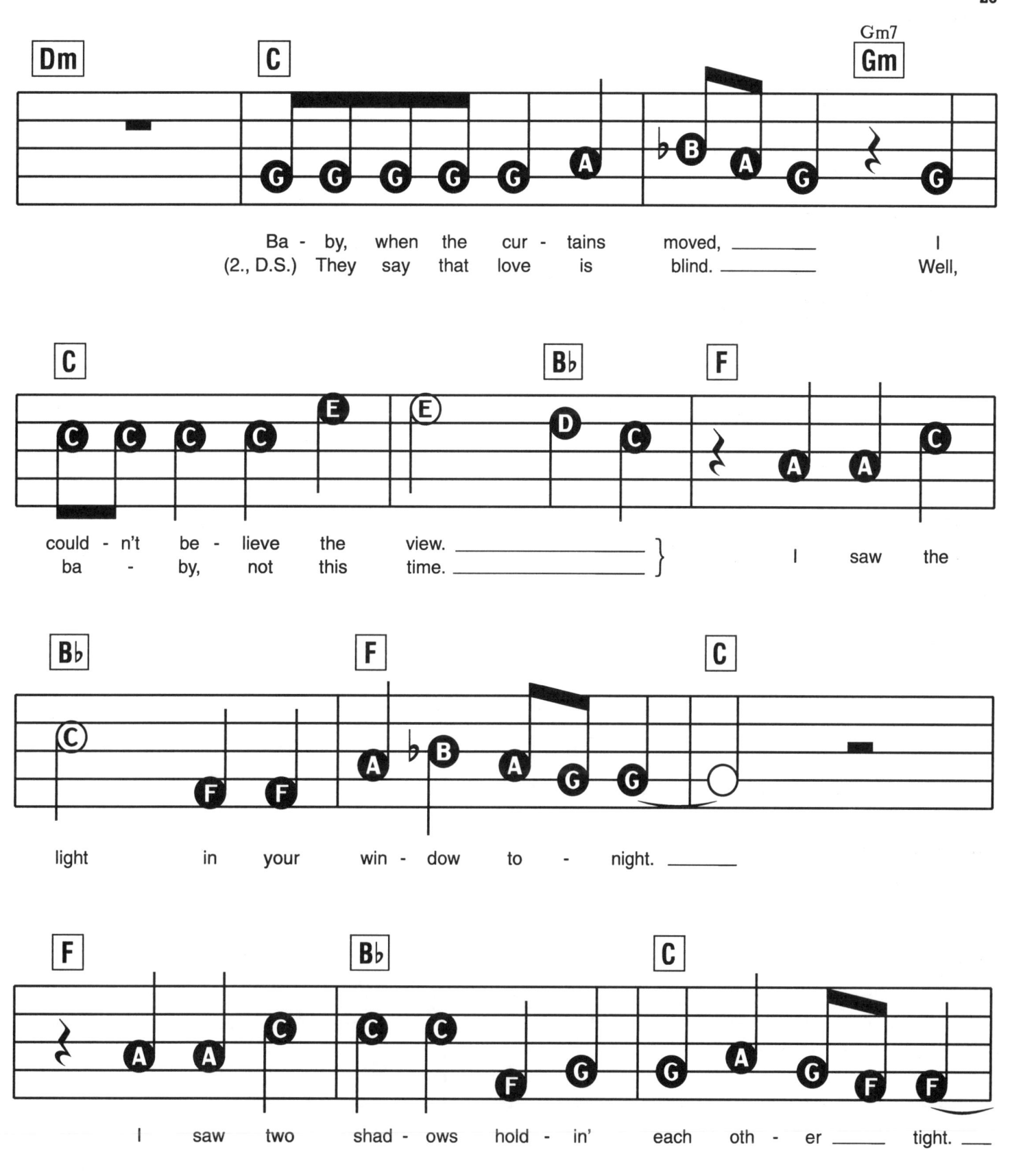

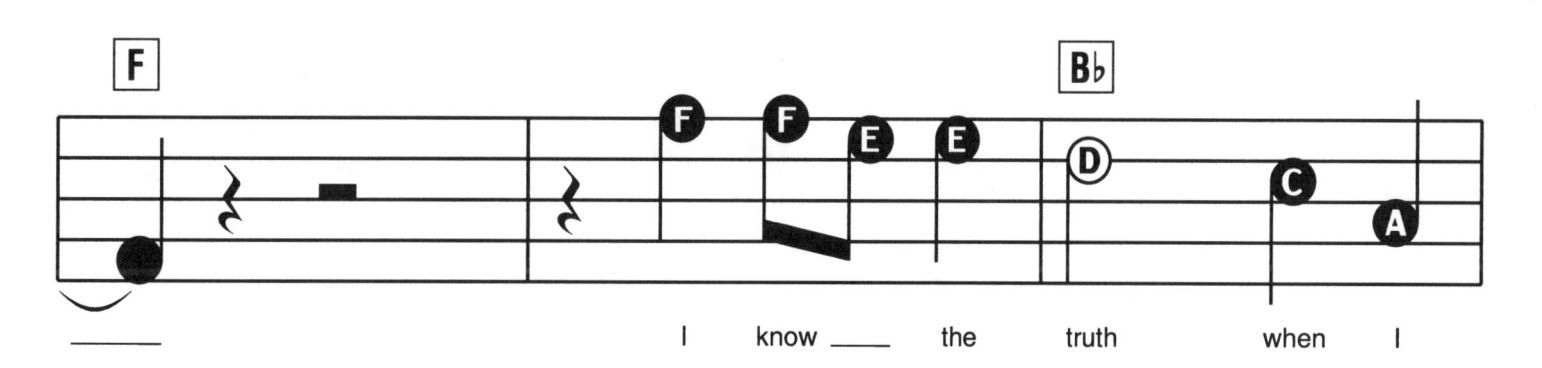

Ba - by, when the cur - tains moved, _____ I
(2., D.S.) They say that love is blind. _____ Well,

could - n't be - lieve the view. _____ ⎫ I saw the
ba - by, not this time. _____ ⎭

light in your win - dow to - night. _____

I saw two shad - ows hold - in' each oth - er _____ tight. ___

_____ I know ___ the truth when I

24

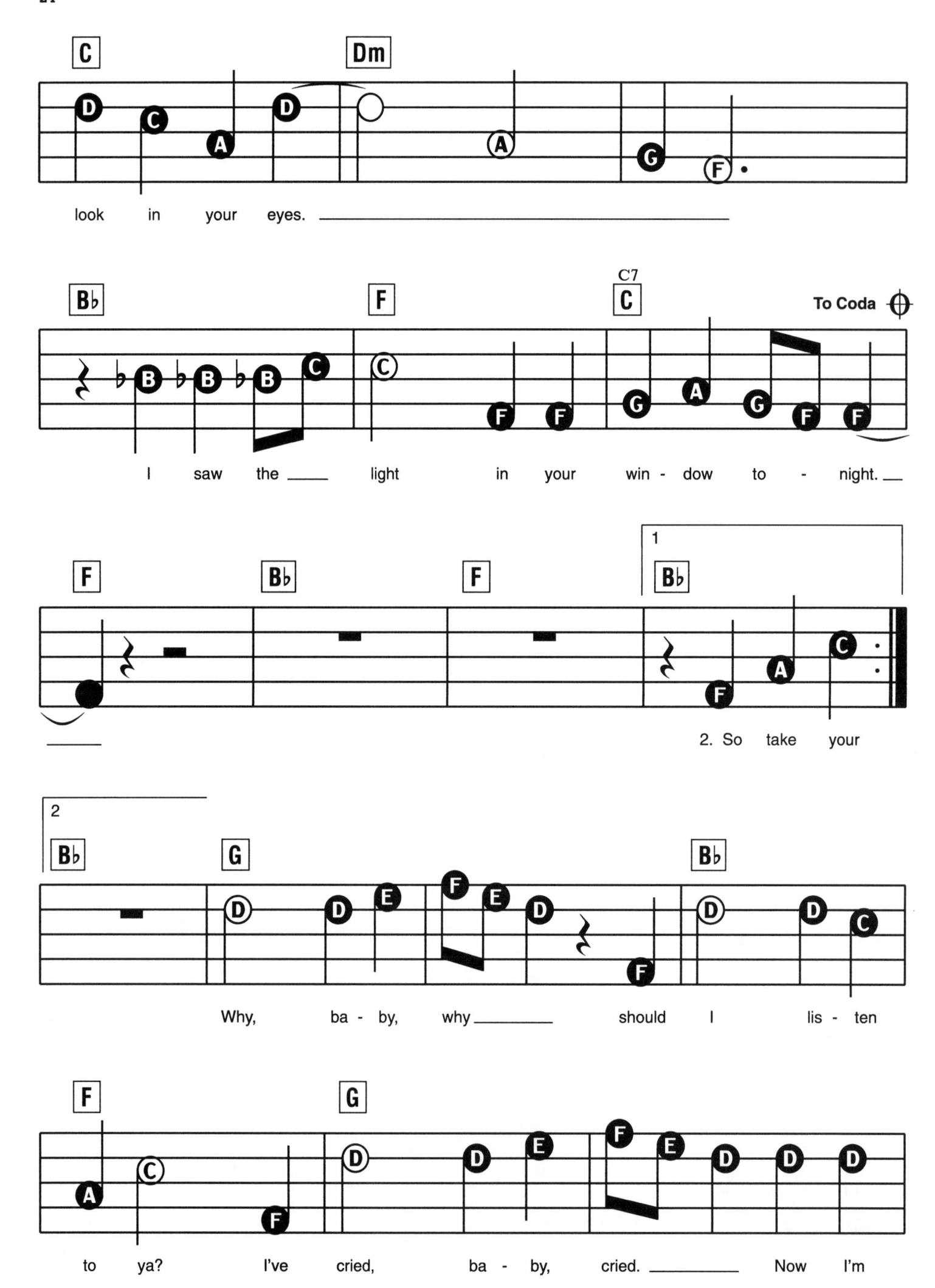

look in your eyes. I saw the light in your win-dow to-night.

2. So take your Why, ba-by, why should I listen to ya? I've cried, ba-by, cried. Now I'm

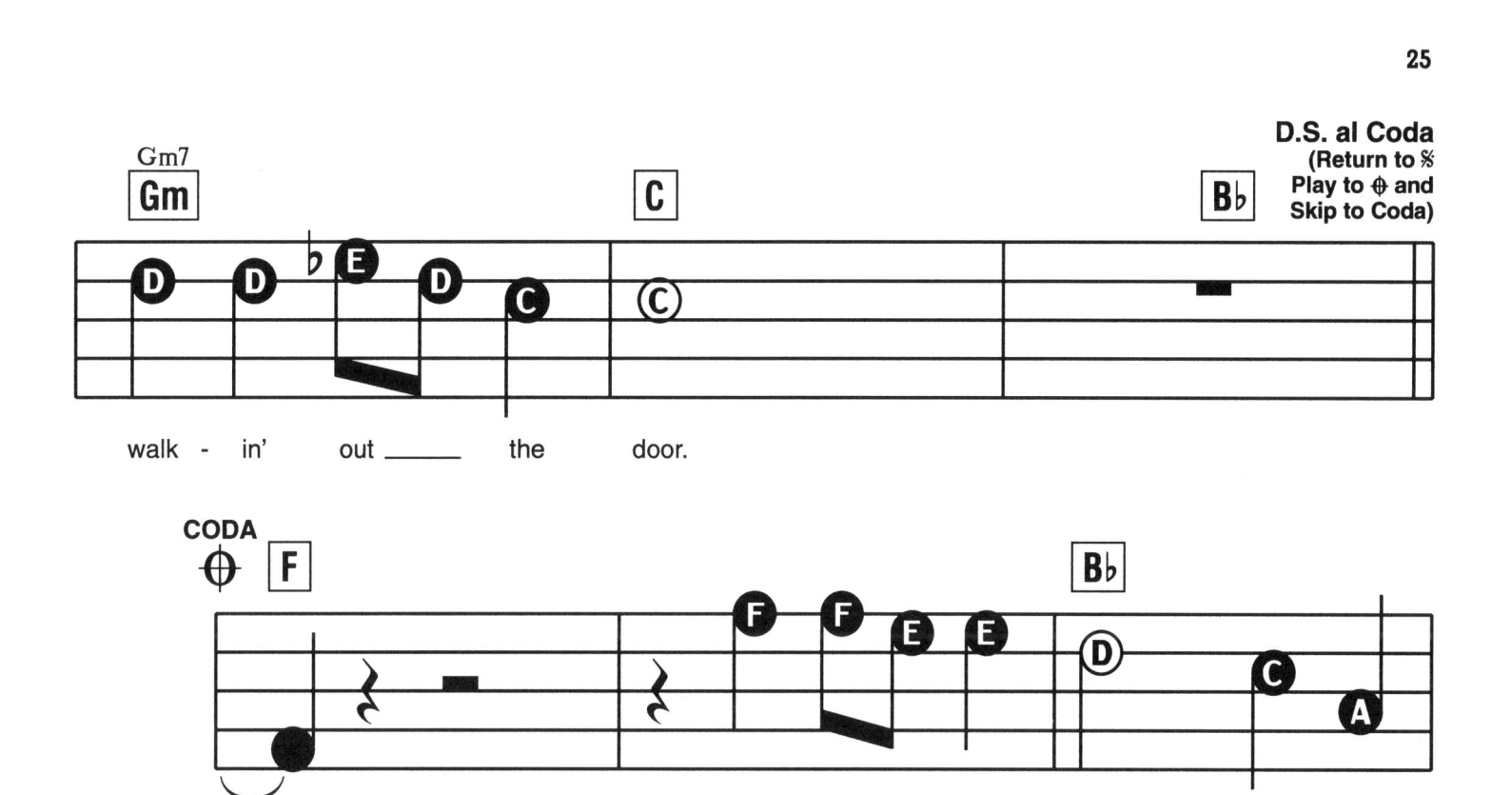

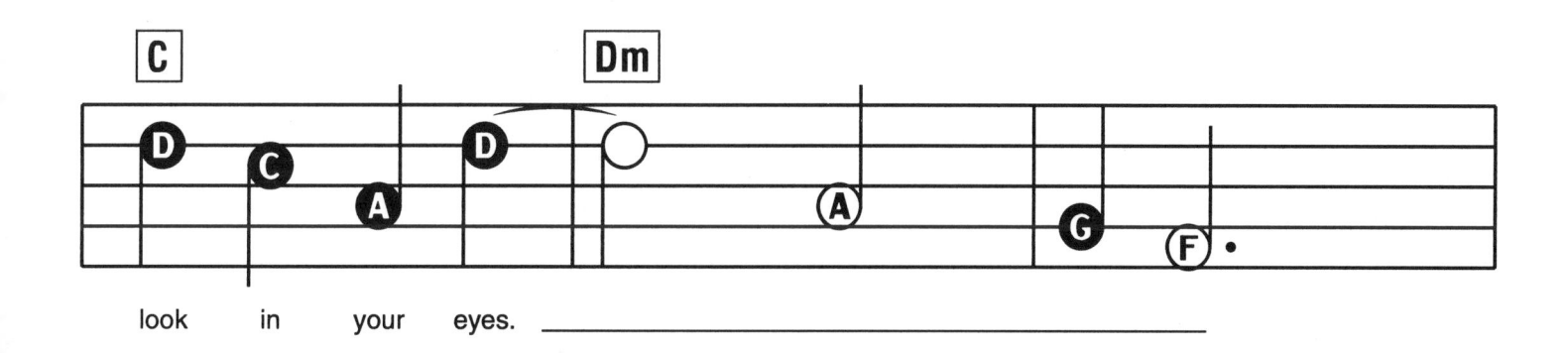

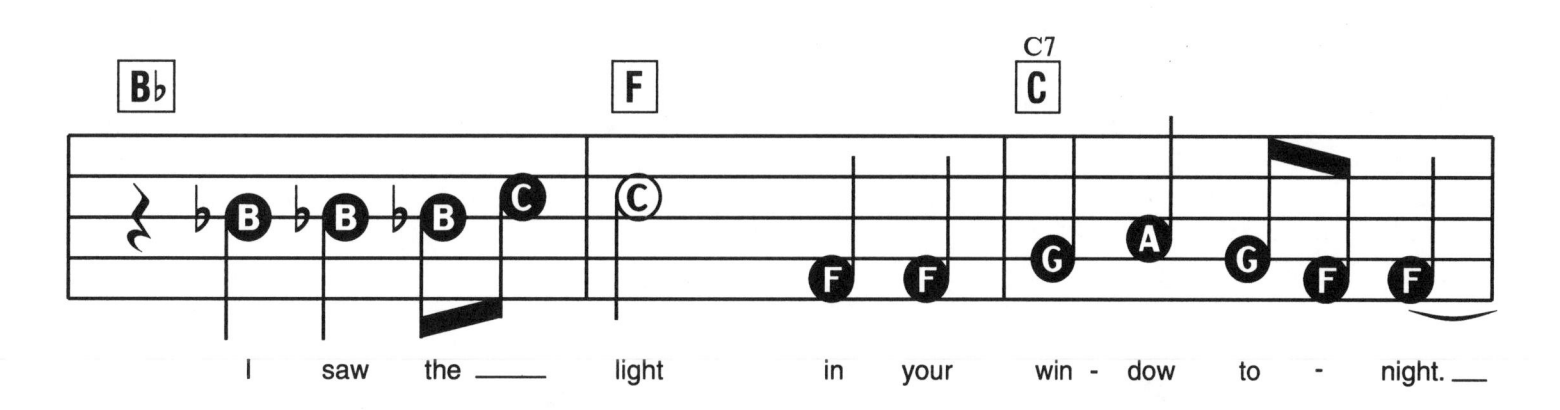

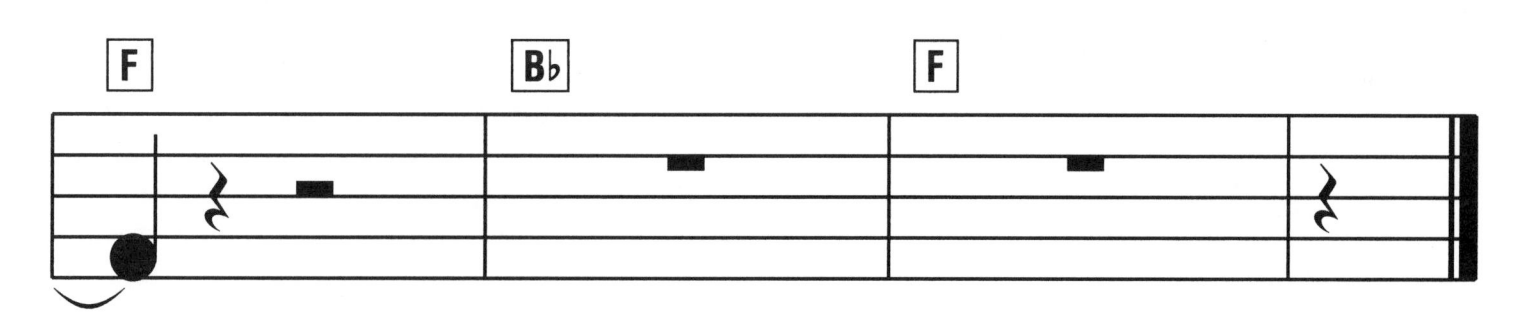

25

walk - in' out ___ the door.

___ I know ___ the truth when I look in your eyes. ___

I saw the ___ light in your win - dow to - night. ___

I Feel Lucky

Registration 5
Rhythm: Blues Rock

Words and Music by Mary-Chapin Carpenter
and Don Schlitz

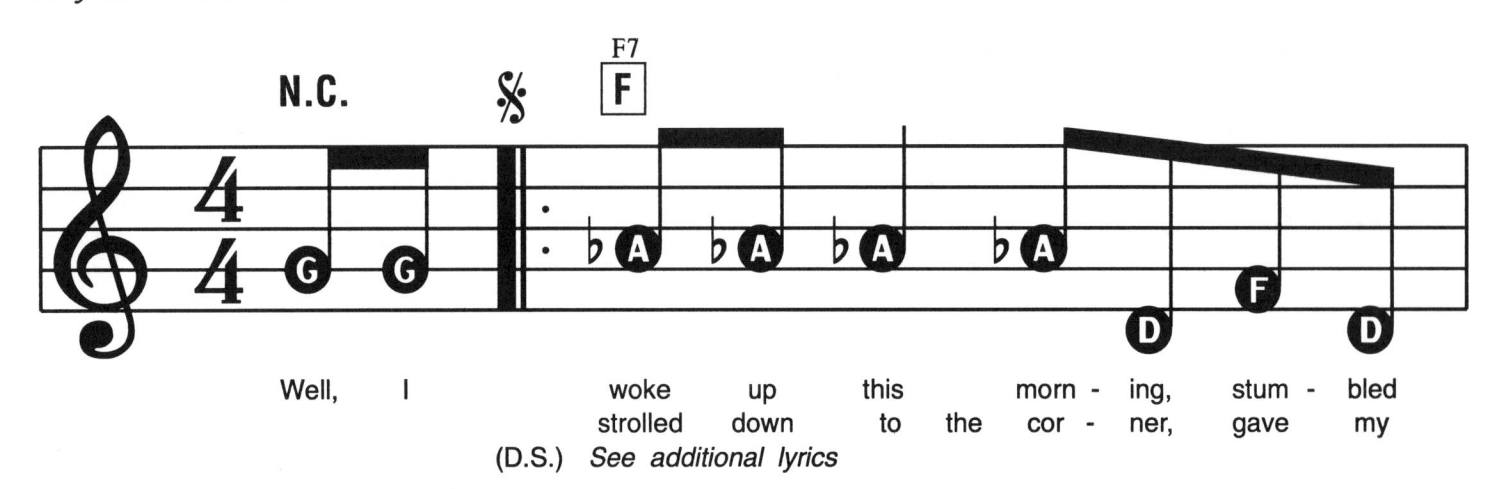

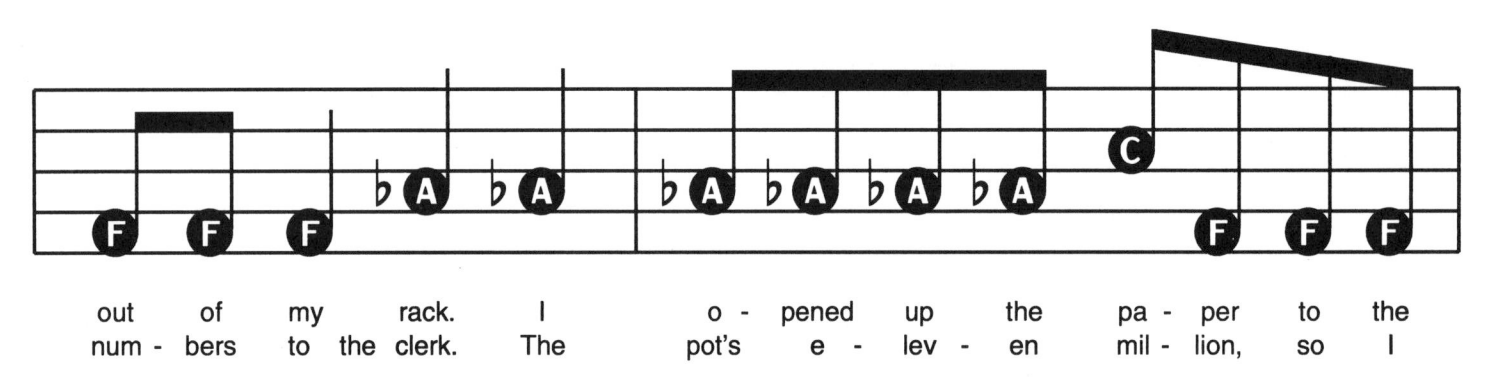

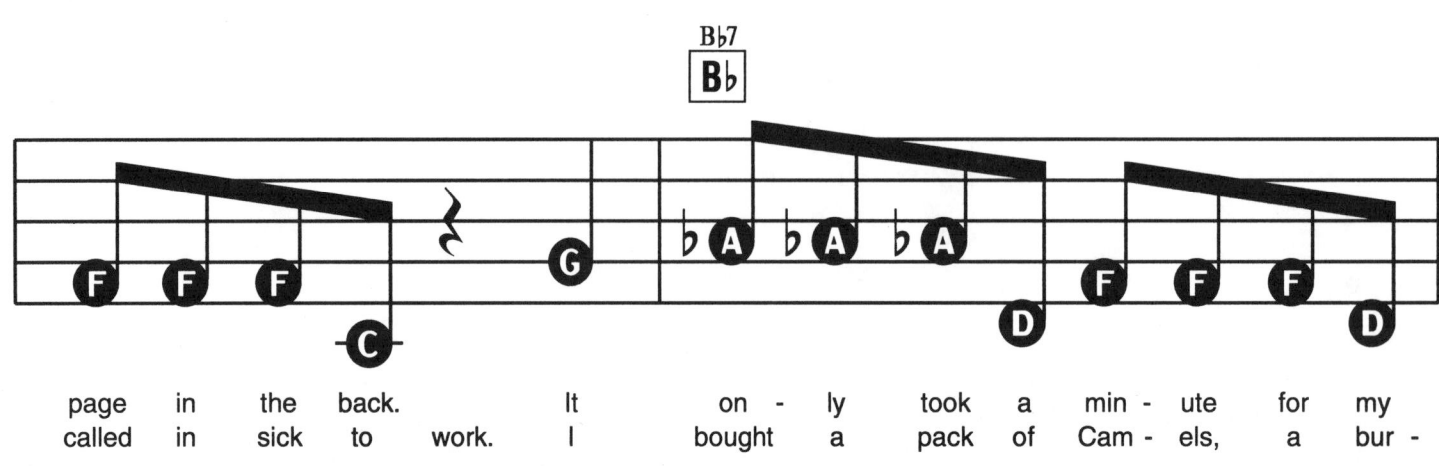

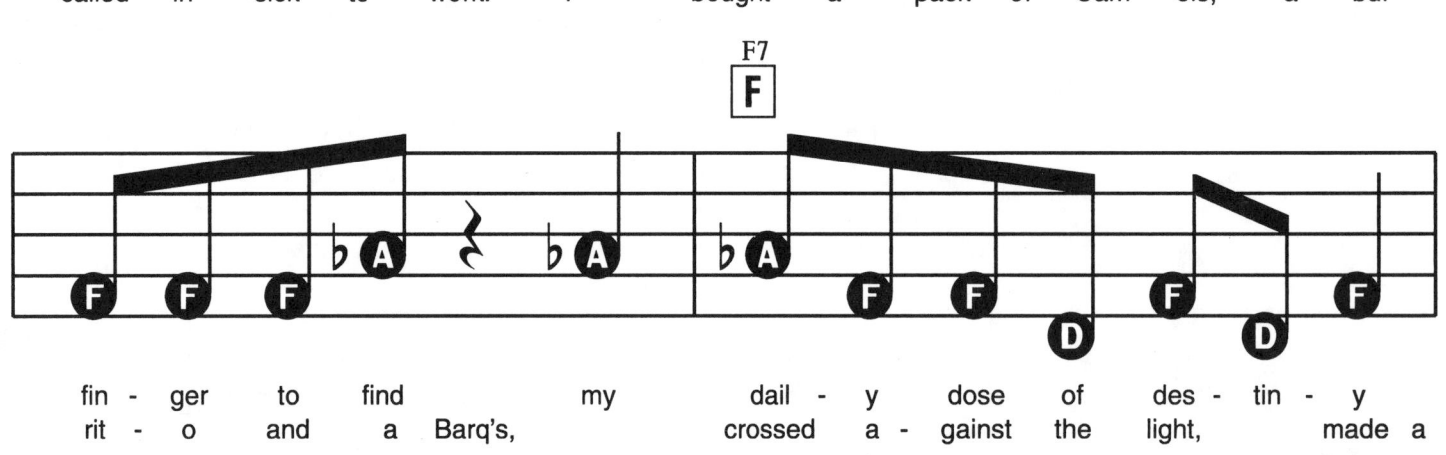

Well, I woke up this morn-ing, stum-bled
strolled down to the cor-ner, gave my

(D.S.) *See additional lyrics*

out of my rack. I o-pened up the pa-per to the
num-bers to the clerk. The pot's e-lev-en mil-lion, so I

page in the back. It on-ly took a min-ute for my
called in sick to work. I bought a pack of Cam-els, a bur-

fin-ger to find my dai-ly dose of des-ti-ny
ri-to and a Barq's, crossed a-gainst the light, made a

© 1992 EMI APRIL MUSIC INC., GETAREALJOB MUSIC, ALMO MUSIC CORP. and DON SCHLITZ MUSIC
All Rights for GETAREALJOB MUSIC Controlled and Administered by EMI APRIL MUSIC INC.
All Rights Reserved   International Copyright Secured   Used by Permission

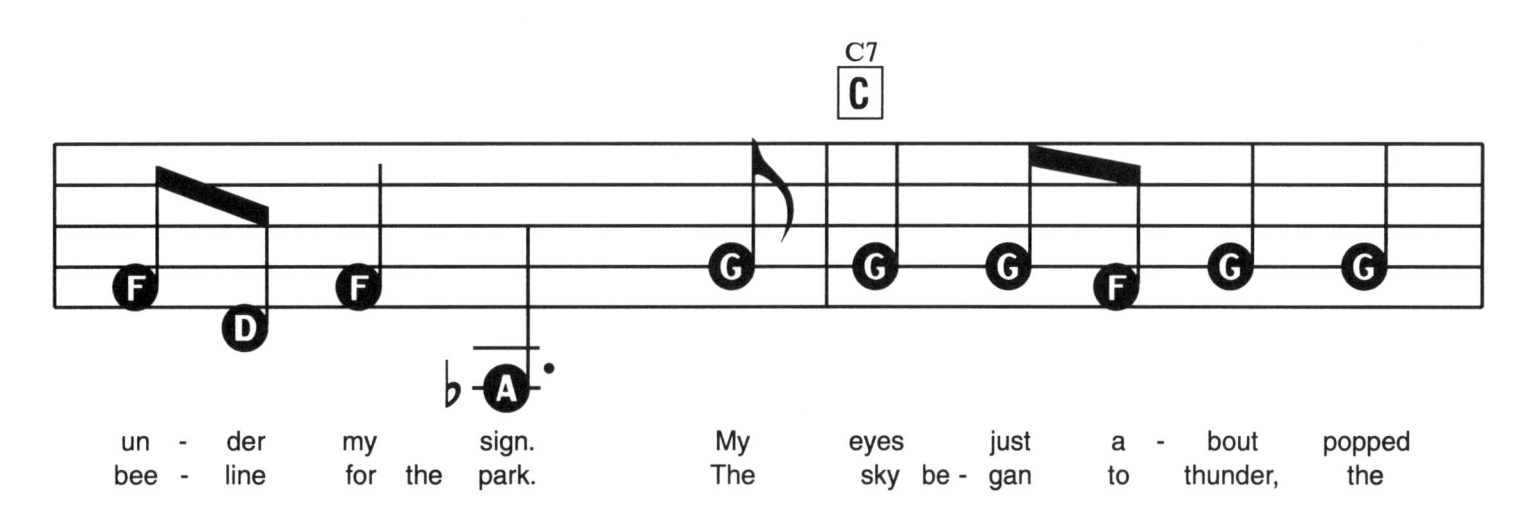

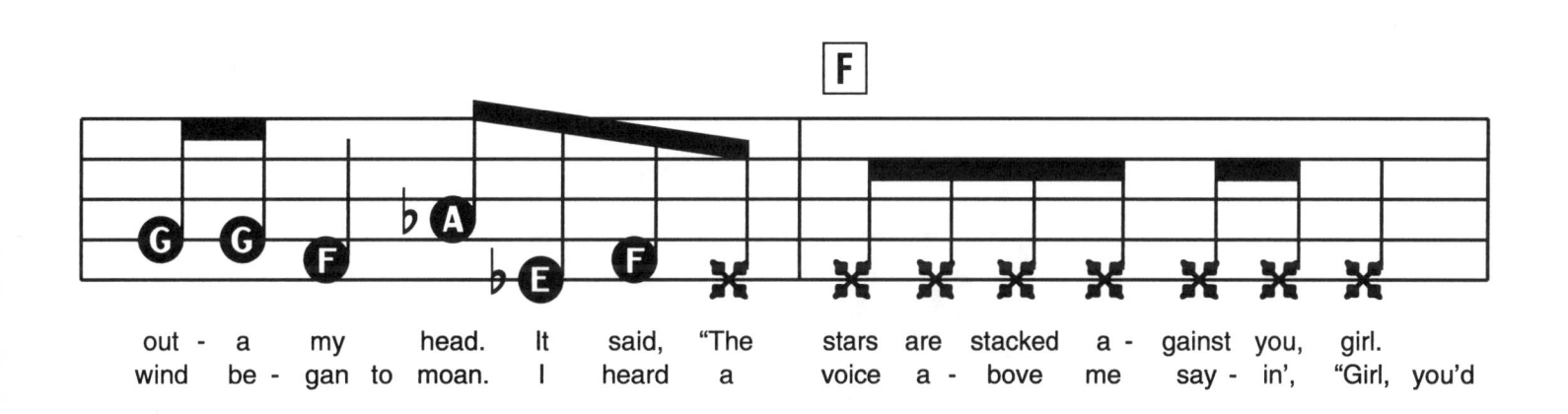

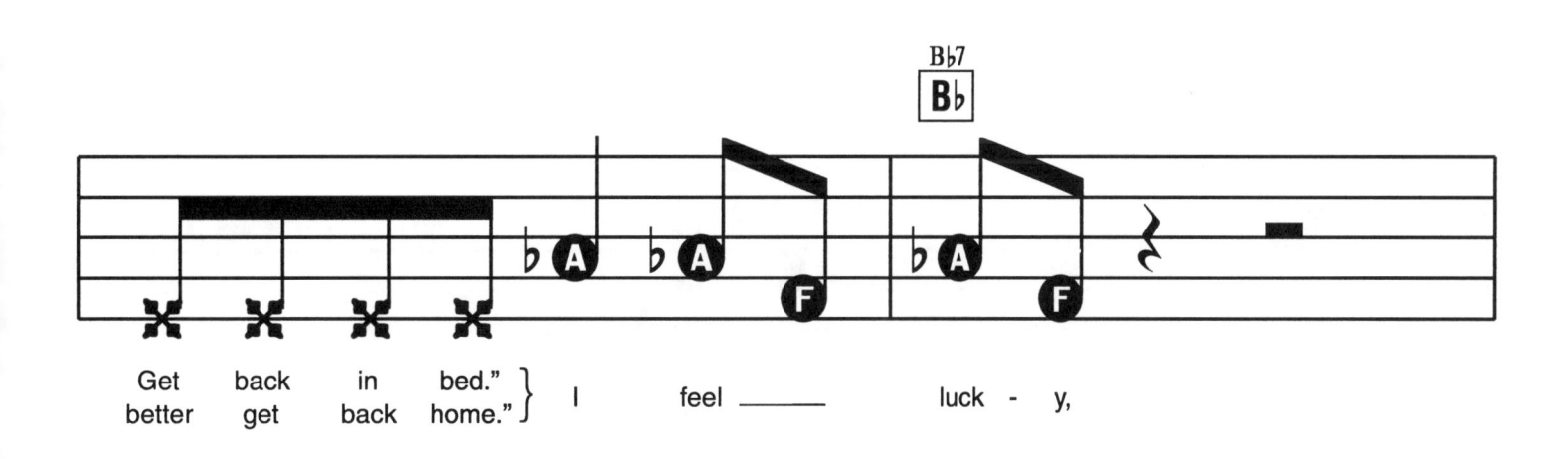

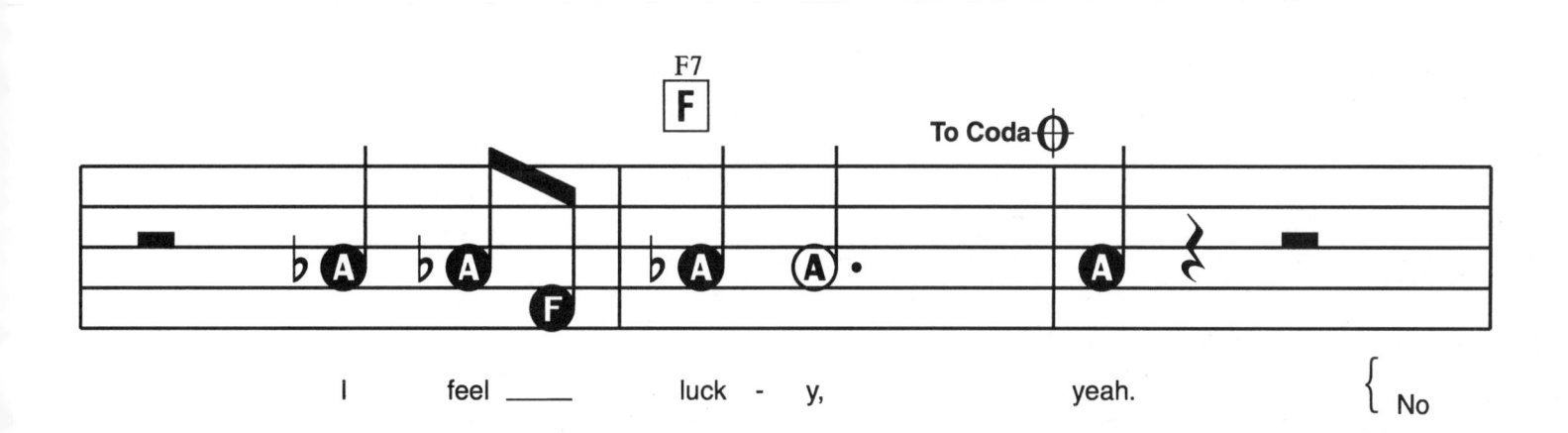

under my sign. My eyes just a - bout popped
bee - line for the park. The sky be - gan to thunder, the

out - a my head. It said, "The stars are stacked a - gainst you, girl.
wind be - gan to moan. I heard a voice a - bove me say - in', "Girl, you'd

Get back in bed." } I feel ____ luck - y,
better get back home."

I feel ____ luck - y, yeah. { No

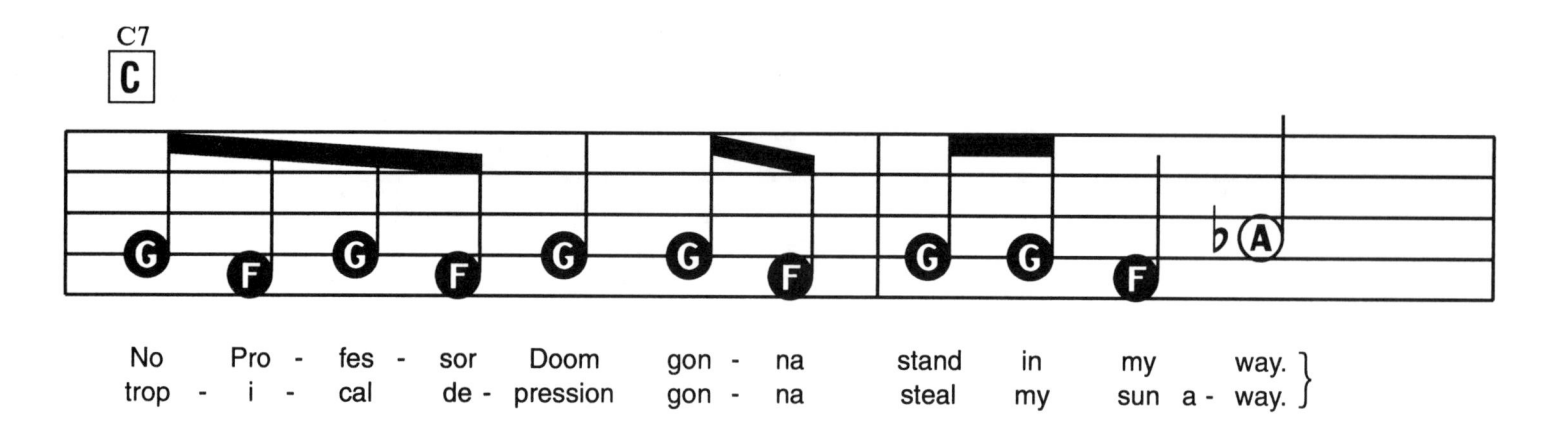

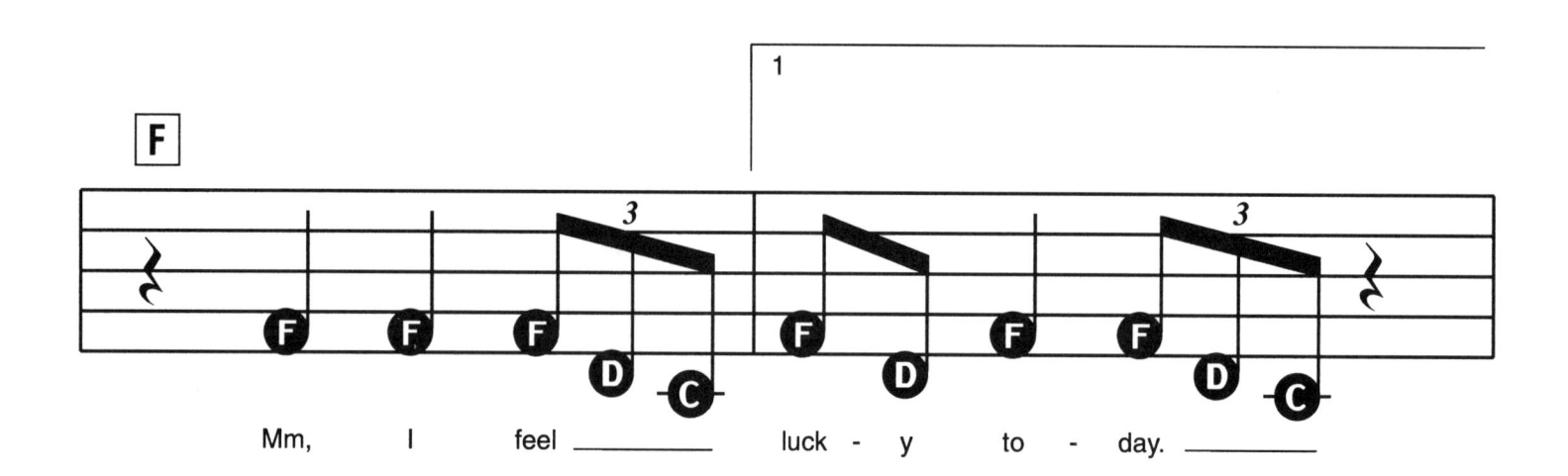

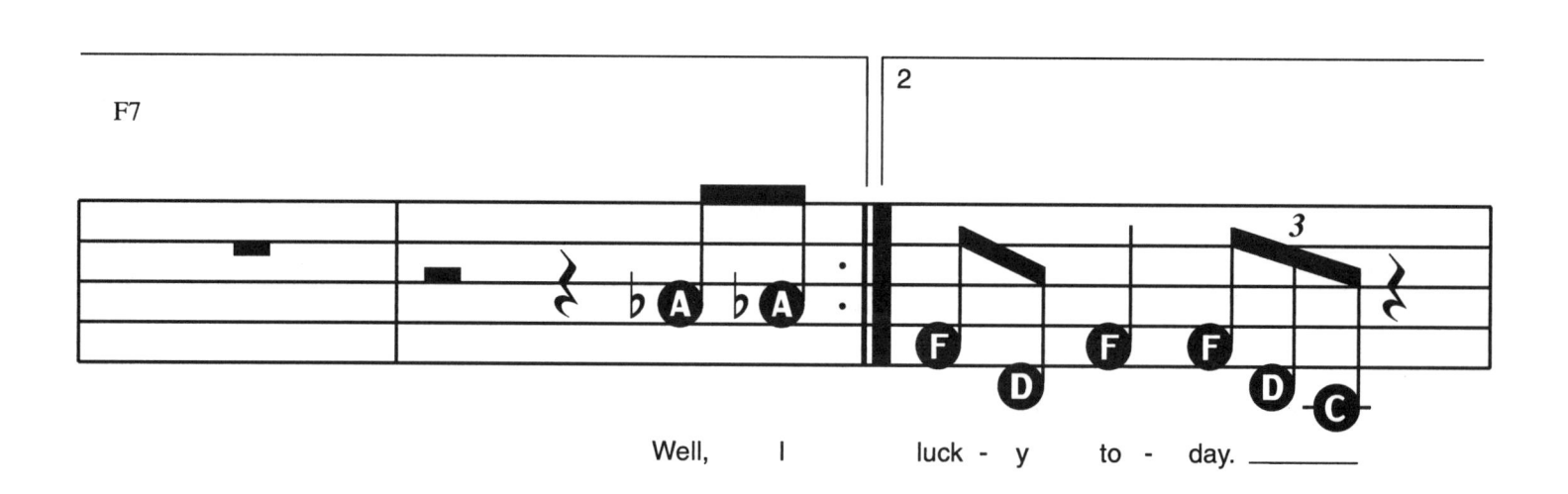

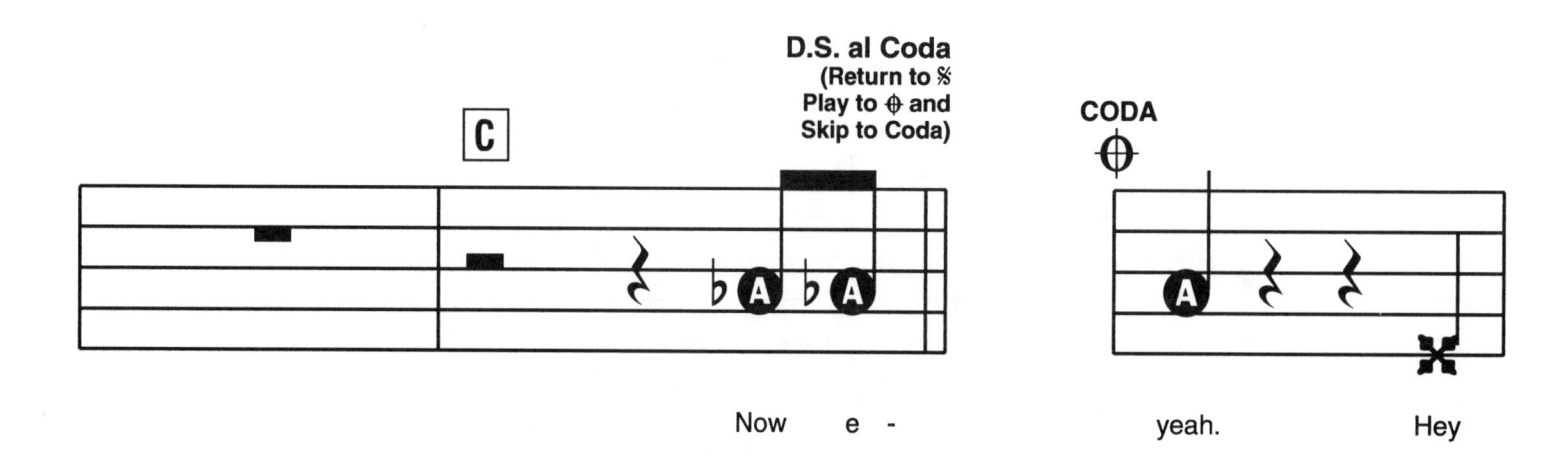

No Professor Doom gonna stand in my way.
tropical depression gonna steal my sun away.

Mm, I feel lucky today.

Well, I lucky today.

D.S. al Coda
(Return to 𝄋
Play to ⊕ and
Skip to Coda)

Now e-

CODA

yeah. Hey

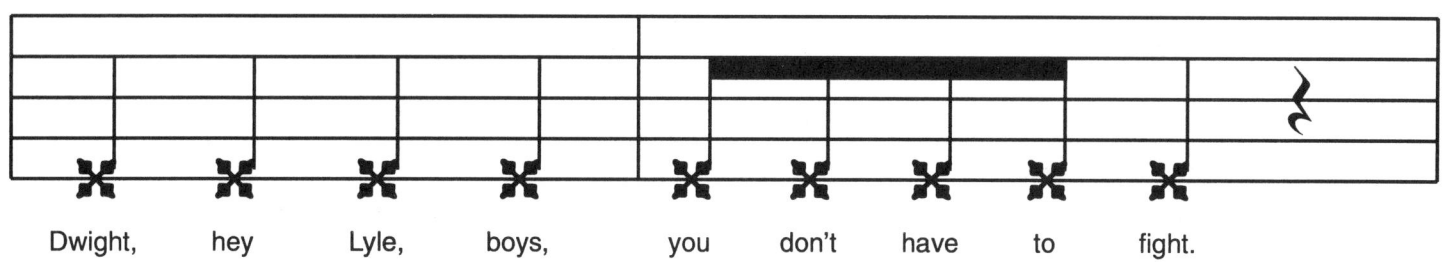

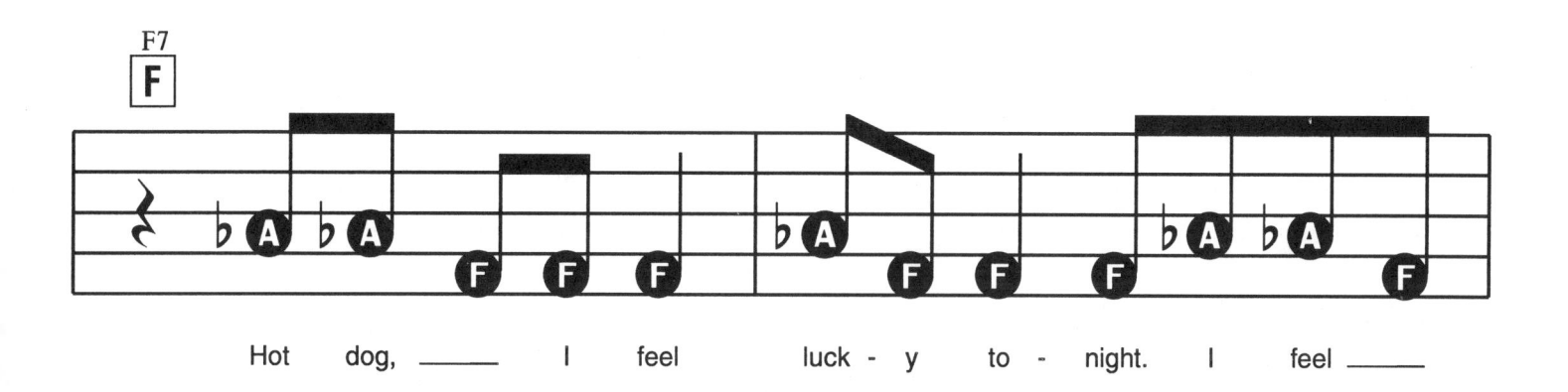

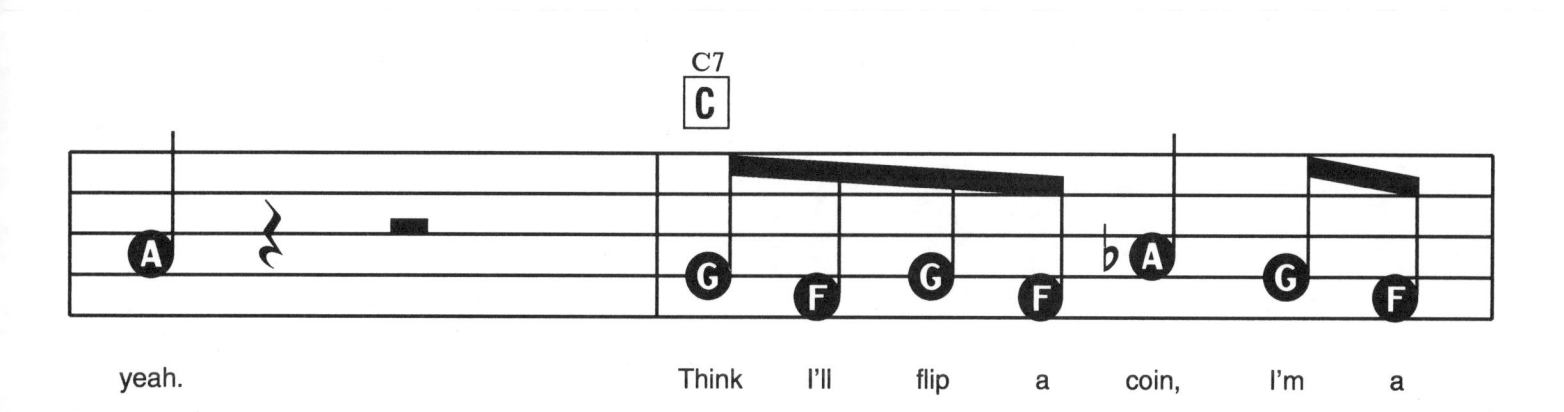

29

Dwight, hey Lyle, boys, you don't have to fight.

Hot dog, _____ I feel luck-y to-night. I feel _____ luck-y, I feel _____ luck-y, yeah. Think I'll flip a coin, I'm a

win - ner ei - ther way. Mm, I feel

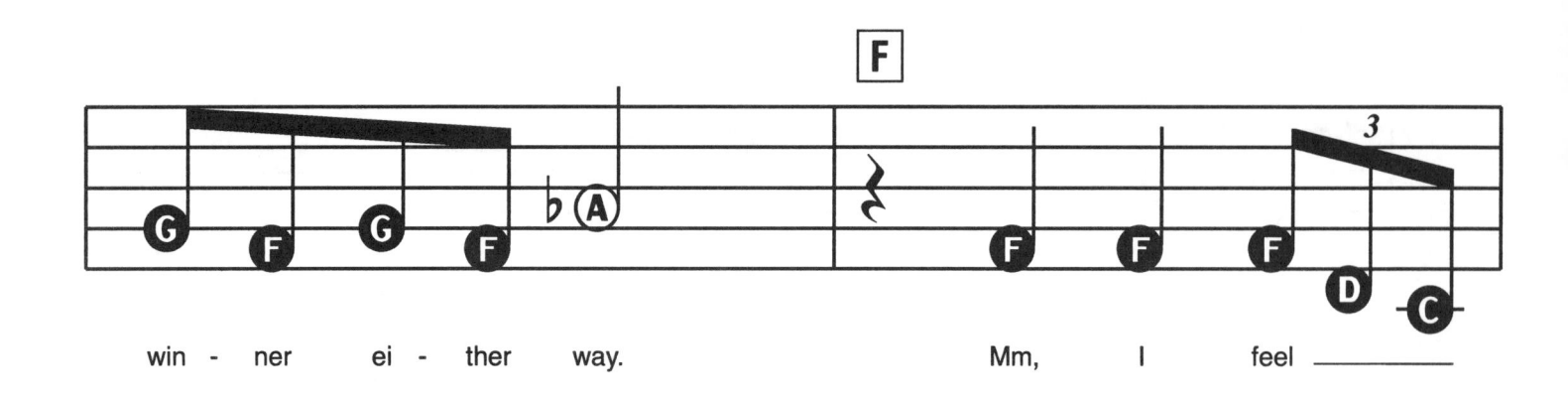

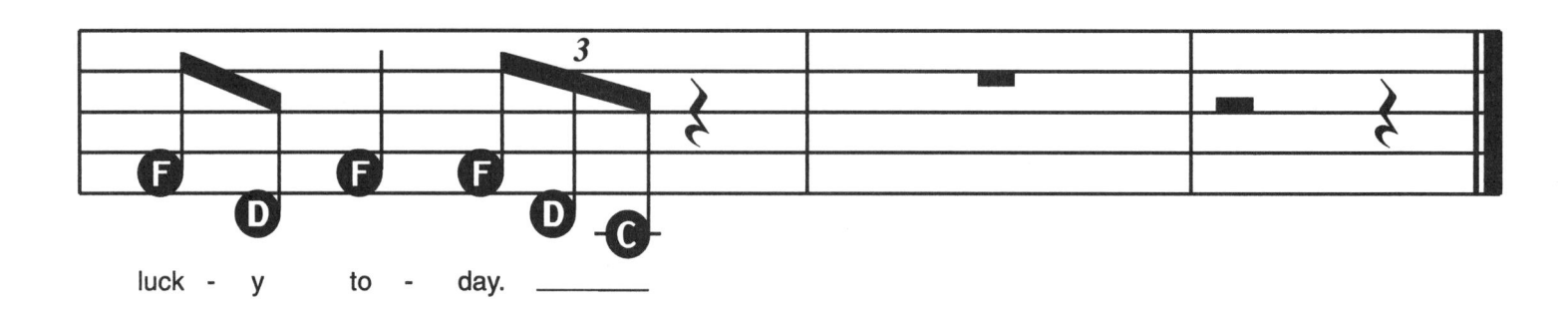

luck - y to - day.

Additional Lyrics

D.S. Now eleven million later, I was sittin' at the bar.
I bought the house a double, then the waitress a new car.
Dwight Yoakim's in the corner, try'n' to catch my eye.
Lyle Lovett's right beside me with his hand upon my thigh.
The moral of this story, it's simple but it's true:
Hey, the stars might lie, but the numbers never do.

Midnight In Montgomery

Registration 3
Rhythm: 8-Beat or Pops

Words and Music by Alan Jackson
and Don Sampson

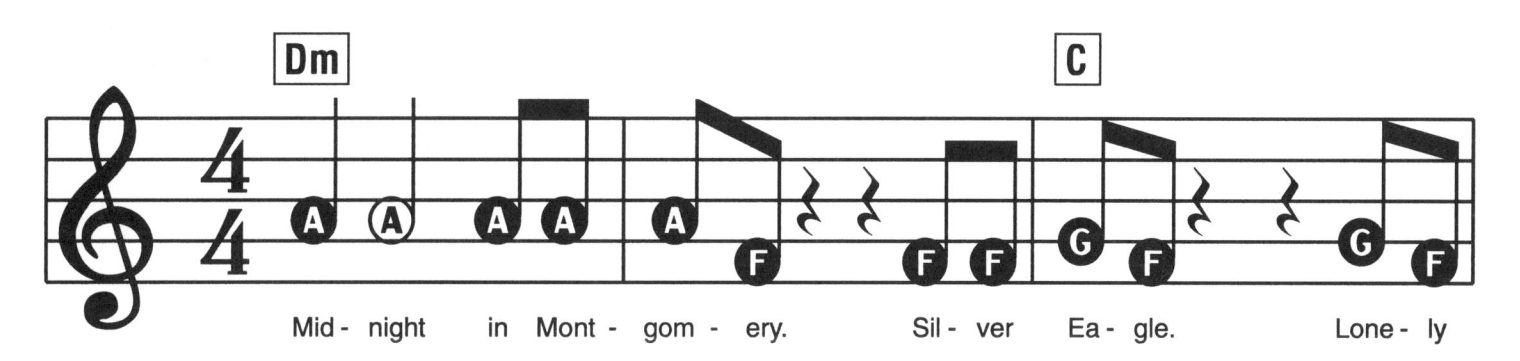

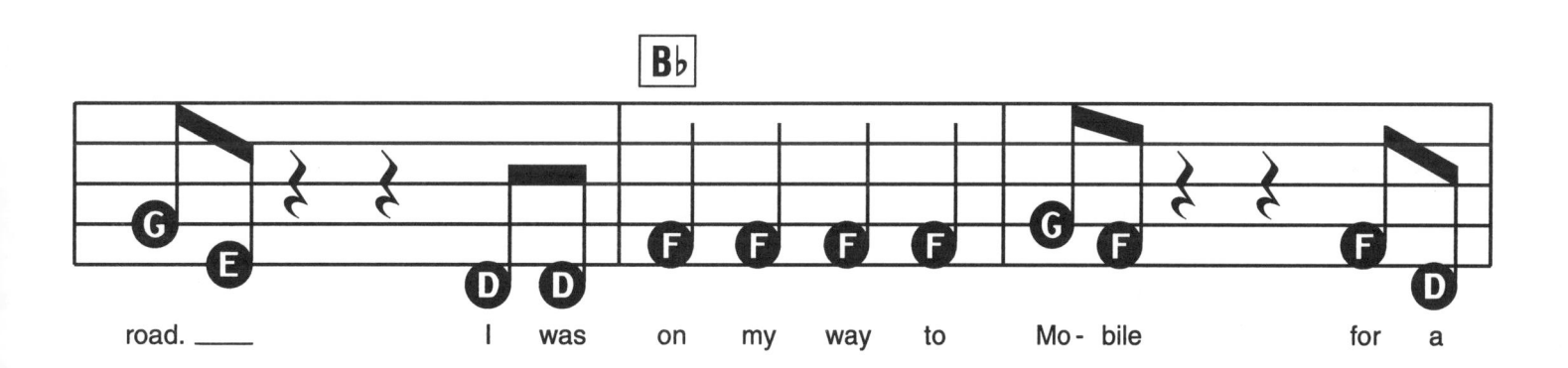

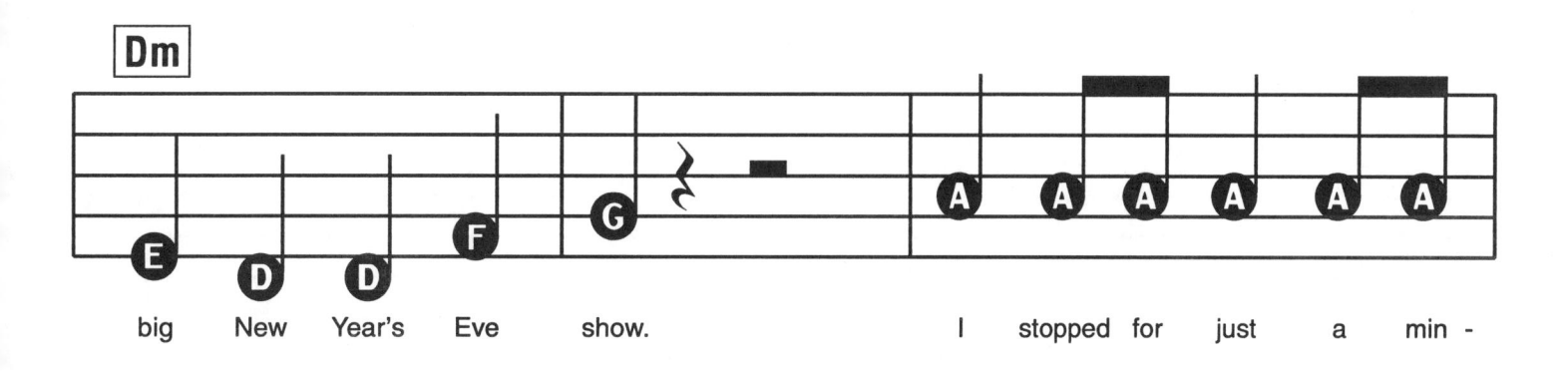

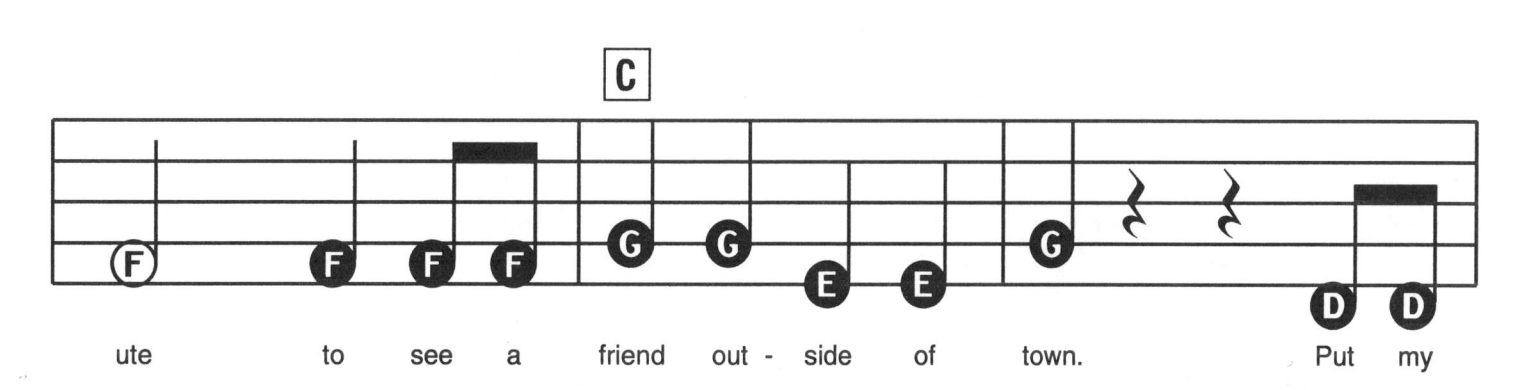

Mid - night in Mont - gom - er - y. Sil - ver Ea - gle. Lone - ly road. ___ I was on my way to Mo - bile for a big New Year's Eve show. I stopped for just a min - ute to see a friend out - side of town. Put my

© 1988, 1991 SEVENTH SON MUSIC, MATTIE RUTH MUSICK and GOLDEN REED MUSIC INC.
All Rights Reserved

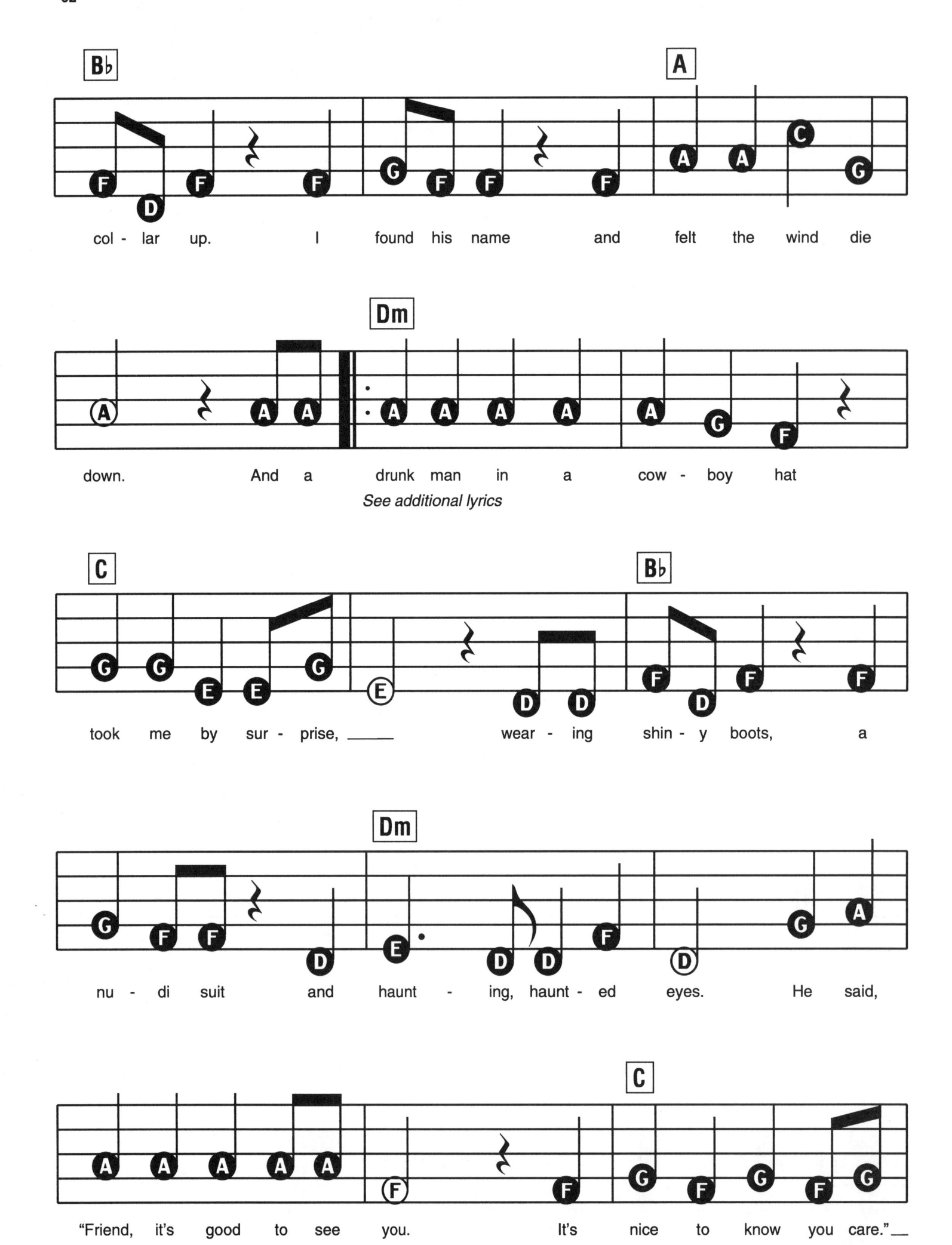

col - lar up. I found his name and felt the wind die down. And a drunk man in a cow - boy hat

See additional lyrics

took me by sur - prise, _____ wear - ing shin - y boots, a nu - di suit and haunt - ing, haunt - ed eyes. He said, "Friend, it's good to see you. It's nice to know you care." _____

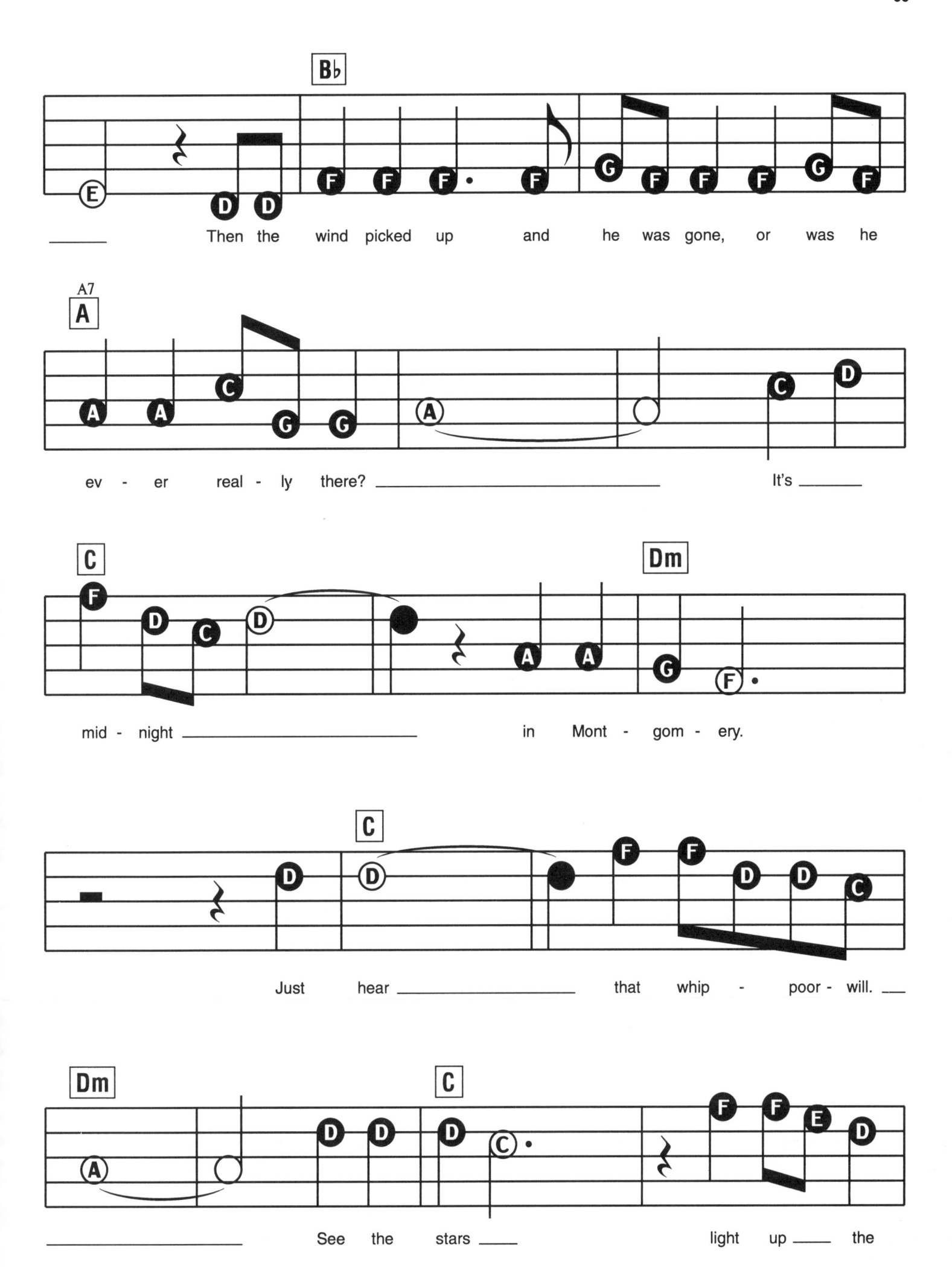

Then the wind picked up and he was gone, or was he ev-er real-ly there? It's mid-night in Mont-gom-ery. Just hear that whip-poor-will. See the stars light up the pur - ple sky, feel _____ that lone - some chill. _____ When the wind is right you'll hear a song, smell whis - key in the air. Mid - night in Mont - gom - ery, he's al - ways sing - ing there.

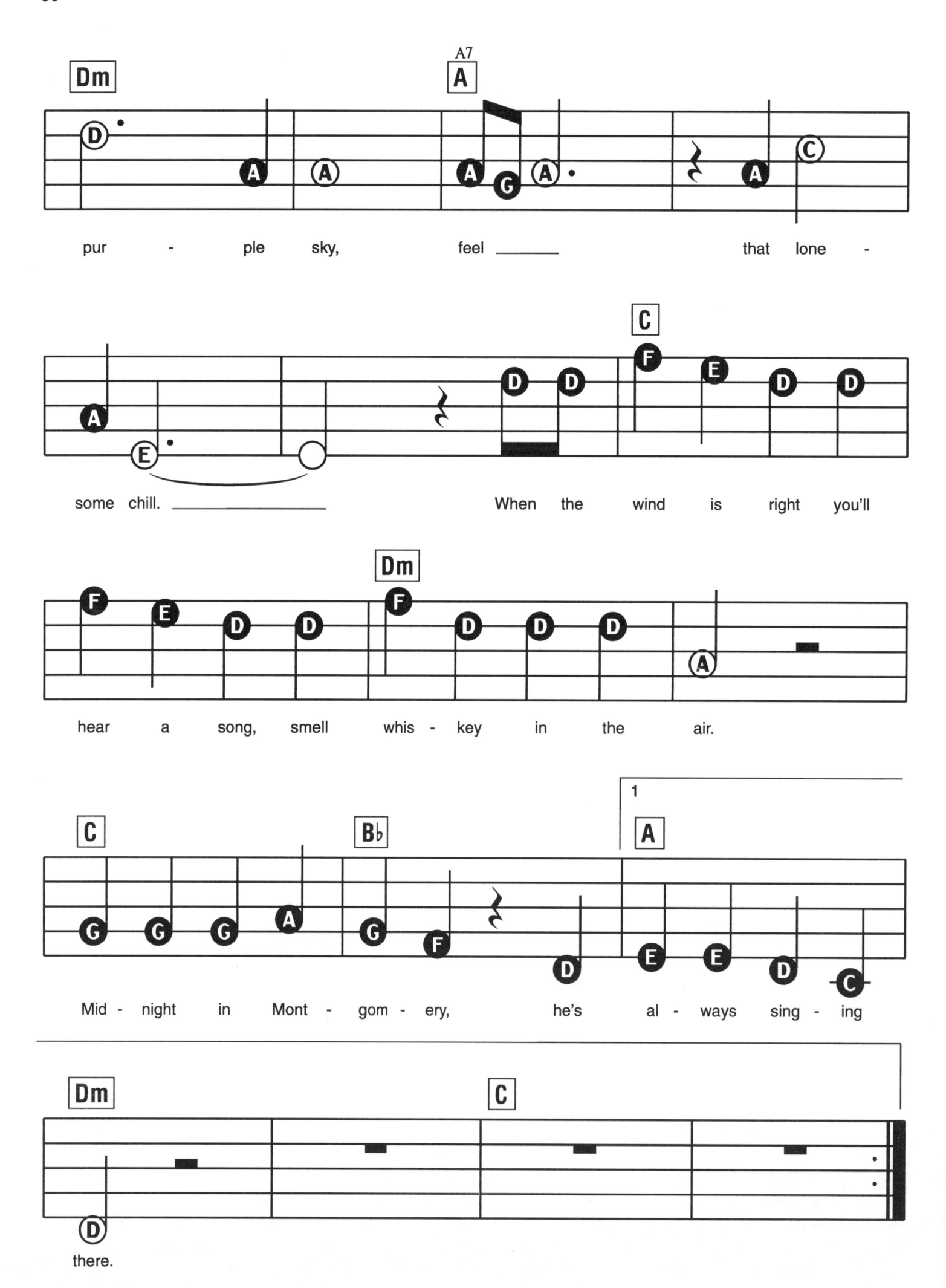

2

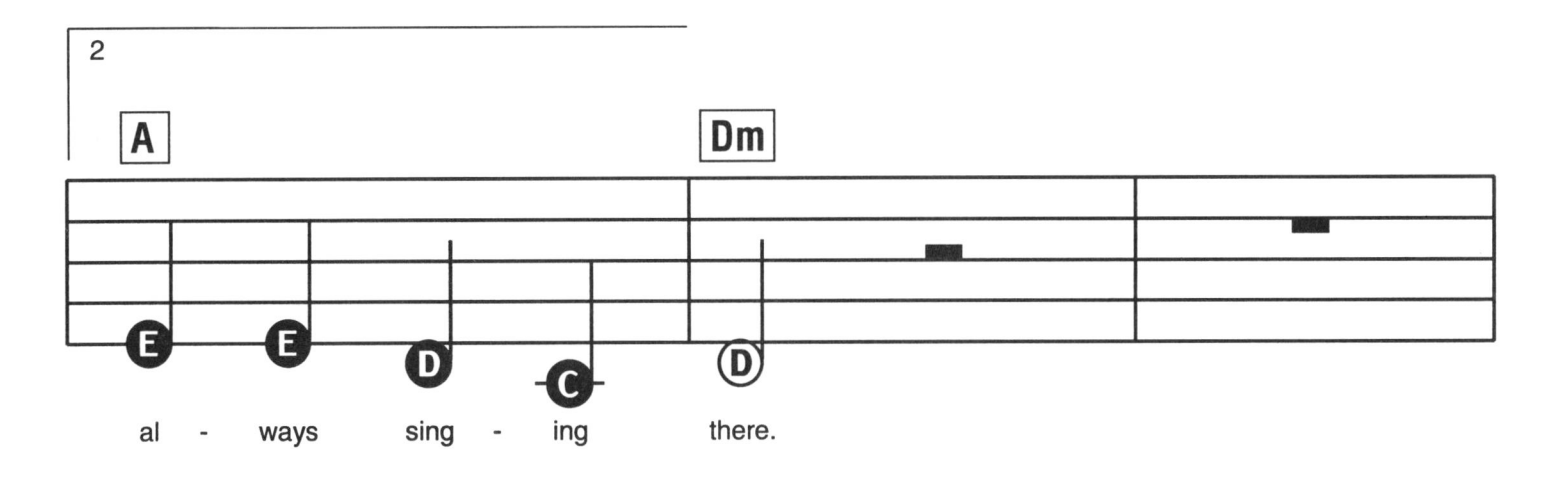

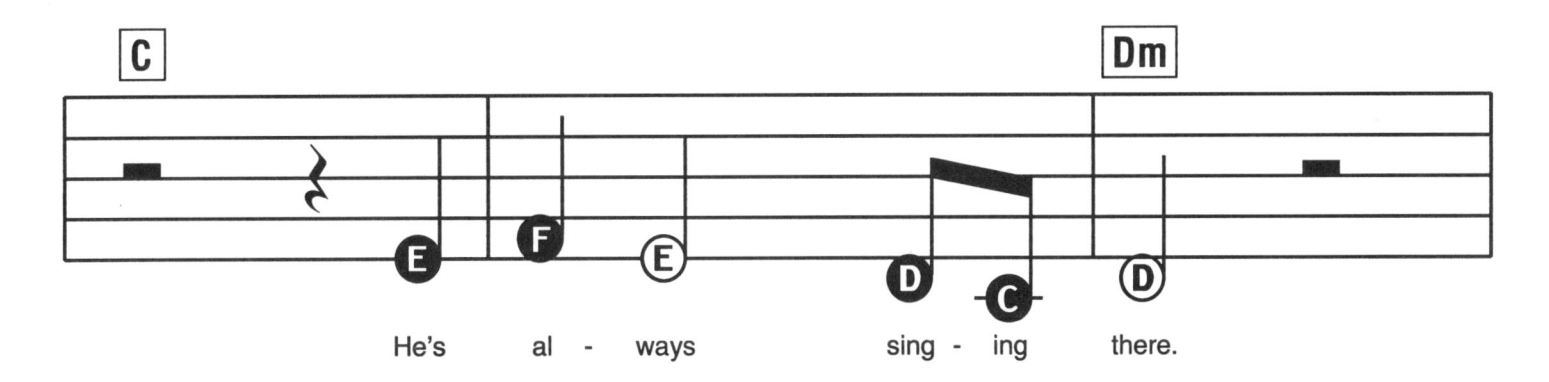

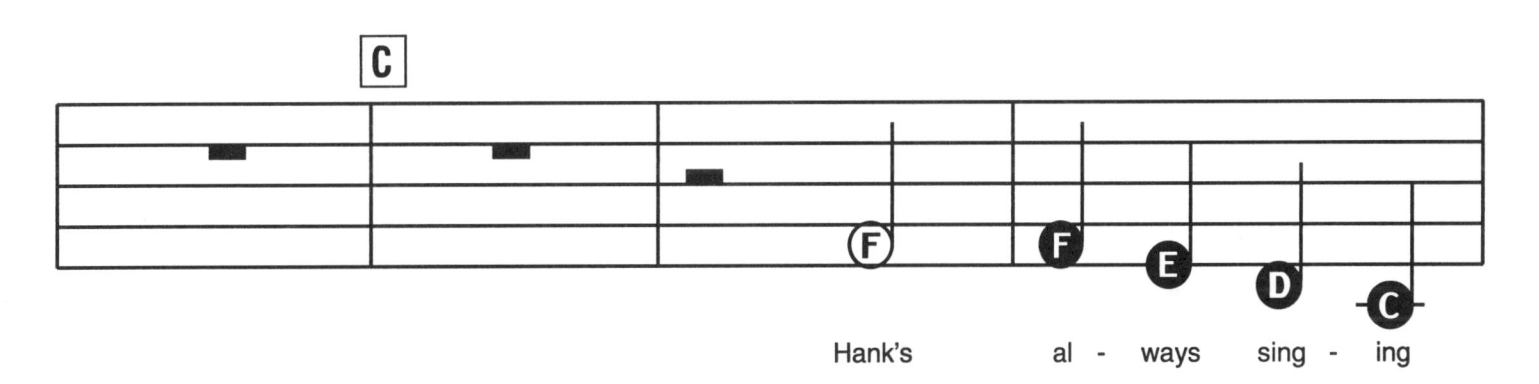

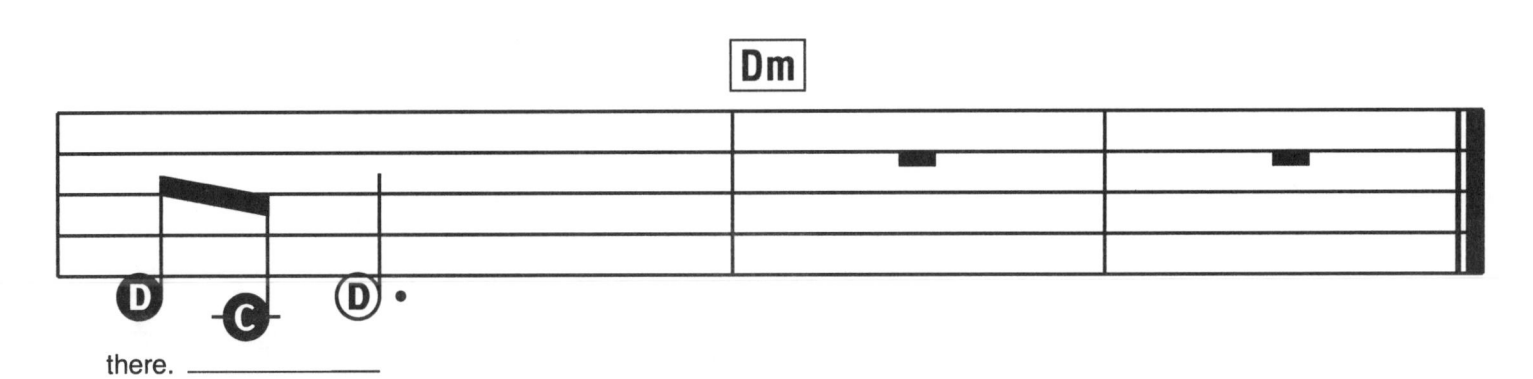

A | **Dm**

E E D C | D |

al - ways sing - ing there.

C | | **Dm**

E F E D C | D

He's al - ways sing - ing there.

C | | |

F F E D C

Hank's al - ways sing - ing

Dm

D C D.

there.

Additional Lyrics

I climbed back on that eagle,
  took one last look around.
The red tail lights, the shadow
  moved slow across the ground.
And off somewhere a midnight train
  is slowly passing by.
I could hear that whistle moaning,
  I'm so lonesome I could cry.

Neon Moon

Registration 1
Rhythm: Pops or 8-Beat

Words and Music by
Ronnie Dunn

When the sun goes down on my side of town that
two young lov-ers running wild and free. I
Instrumental solo

lone - some feel-ing comes to my door and the
close my eyes and some - times see

whole world turns
you in the shad - ows of this

blue.
smoke - filled room.
Solo ends

There's a
No tell - ing
The

Copyright © 1990 Tree Publishing Co., Inc.
All rights administered by Sony Music Publishing, 8 Music Square West, Nashville, TN 37203
International Copyright Secured All Rights Reserved

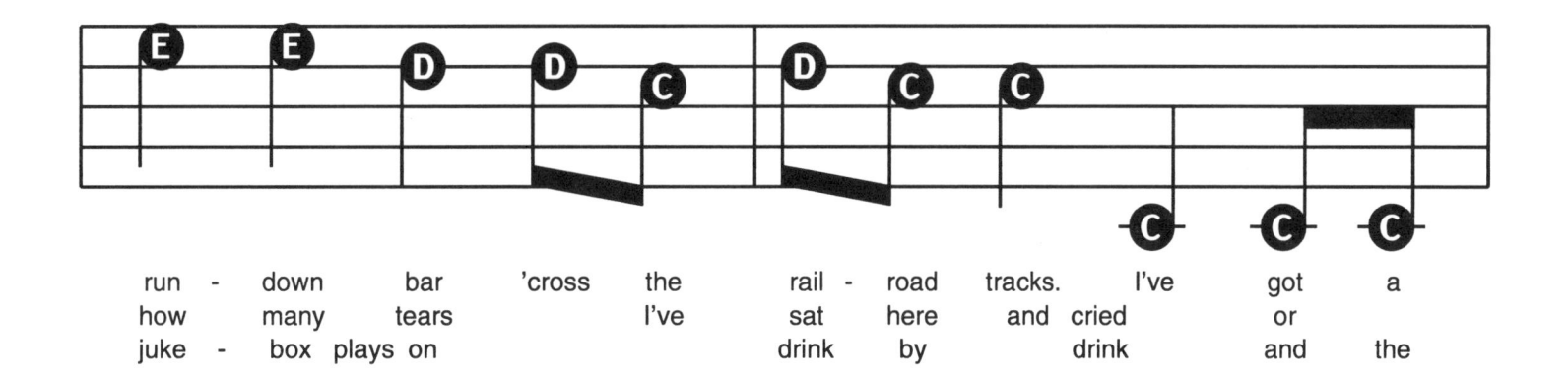

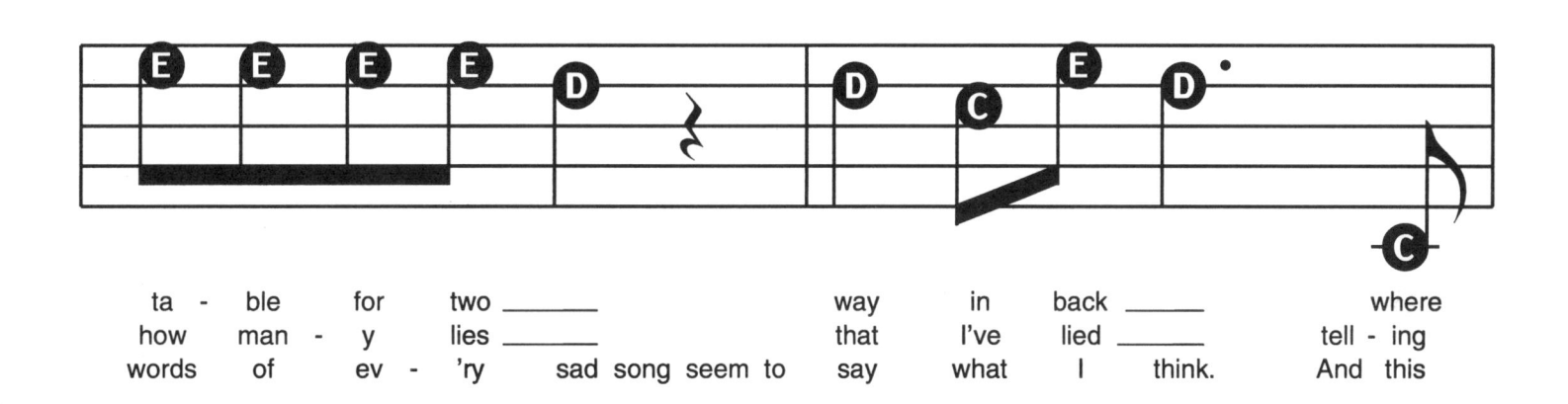

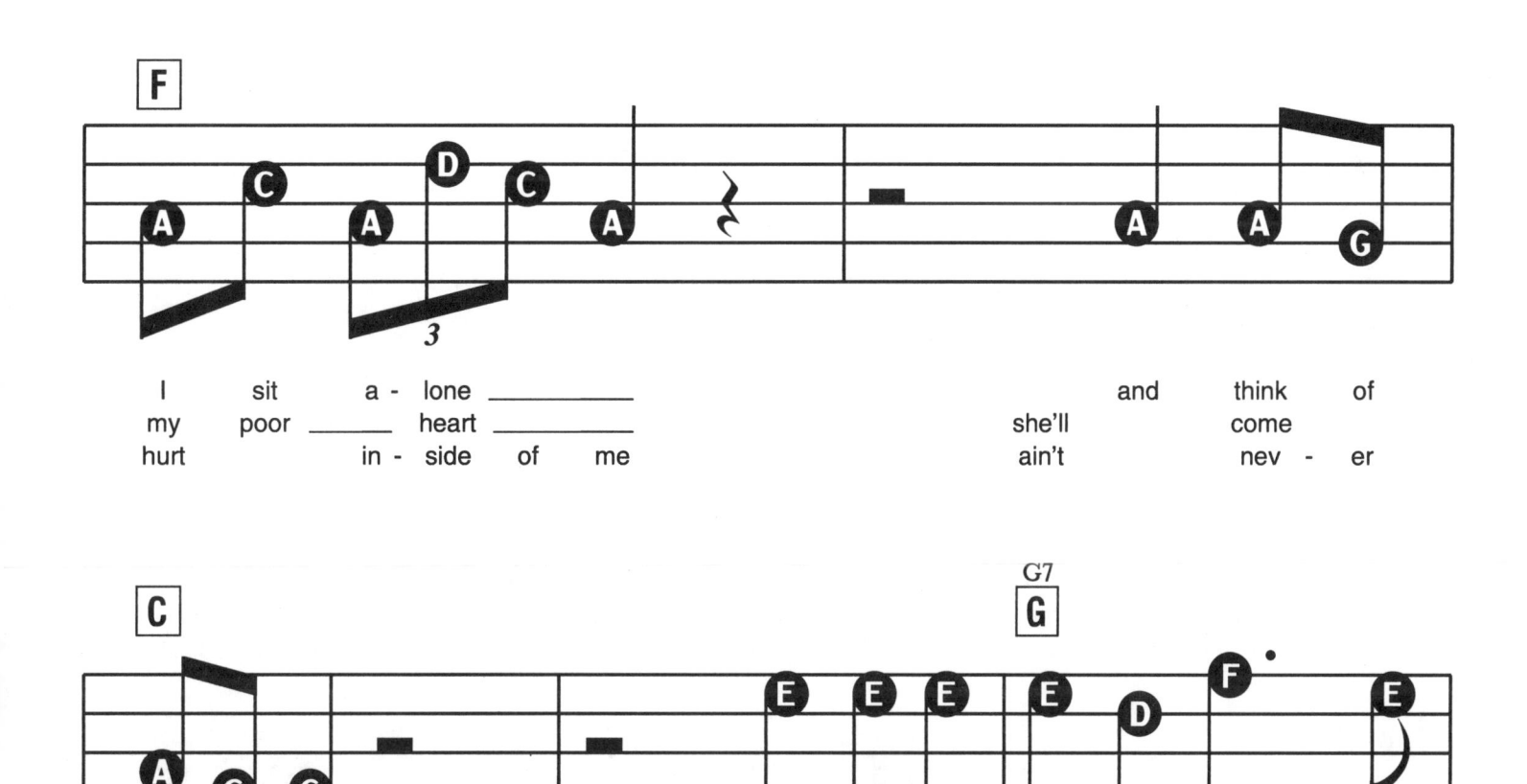

run - down bar 'cross the rail - road tracks. I've got a
how many tears I've sat here and cried or
juke - box plays on drink by drink and the

ta - ble for two way in back where
how man - y lies that I've lied tell - ing
words of ev - 'ry sad song seem to say what I think. And this

[F]
I sit a - lone and think of
my poor heart she'll come
hurt in - side of me ain't nev - er

[C]   [G] G7
los - ing you.   I spend most ev - 'ry night be -
back some - day.   Oh, but I'll be al - right as
gon - na end.   Oh, but I'll be al - right as

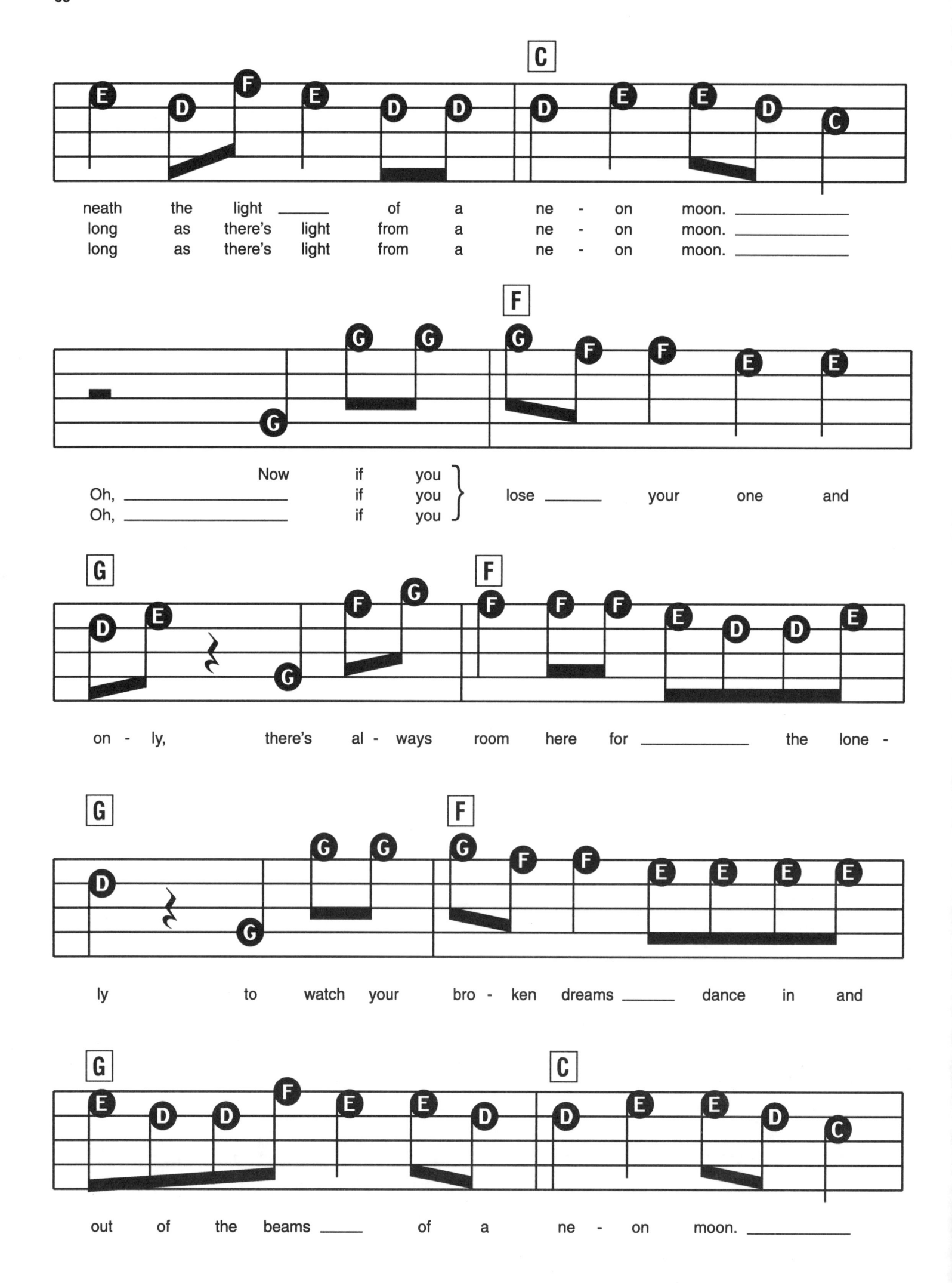

neath the light _____ of a ne - on moon. _____
long as there's light from a ne - on moon. _____
long as there's light from a ne - on moon. _____

Now if you
Oh, _____ if you } lose _____ your one and
Oh, _____ if you

on - ly, there's al - ways room here for _____ the lone -

ly to watch your bro - ken dreams _____ dance in and

out of the beams _____ of a ne - on moon. _____

39

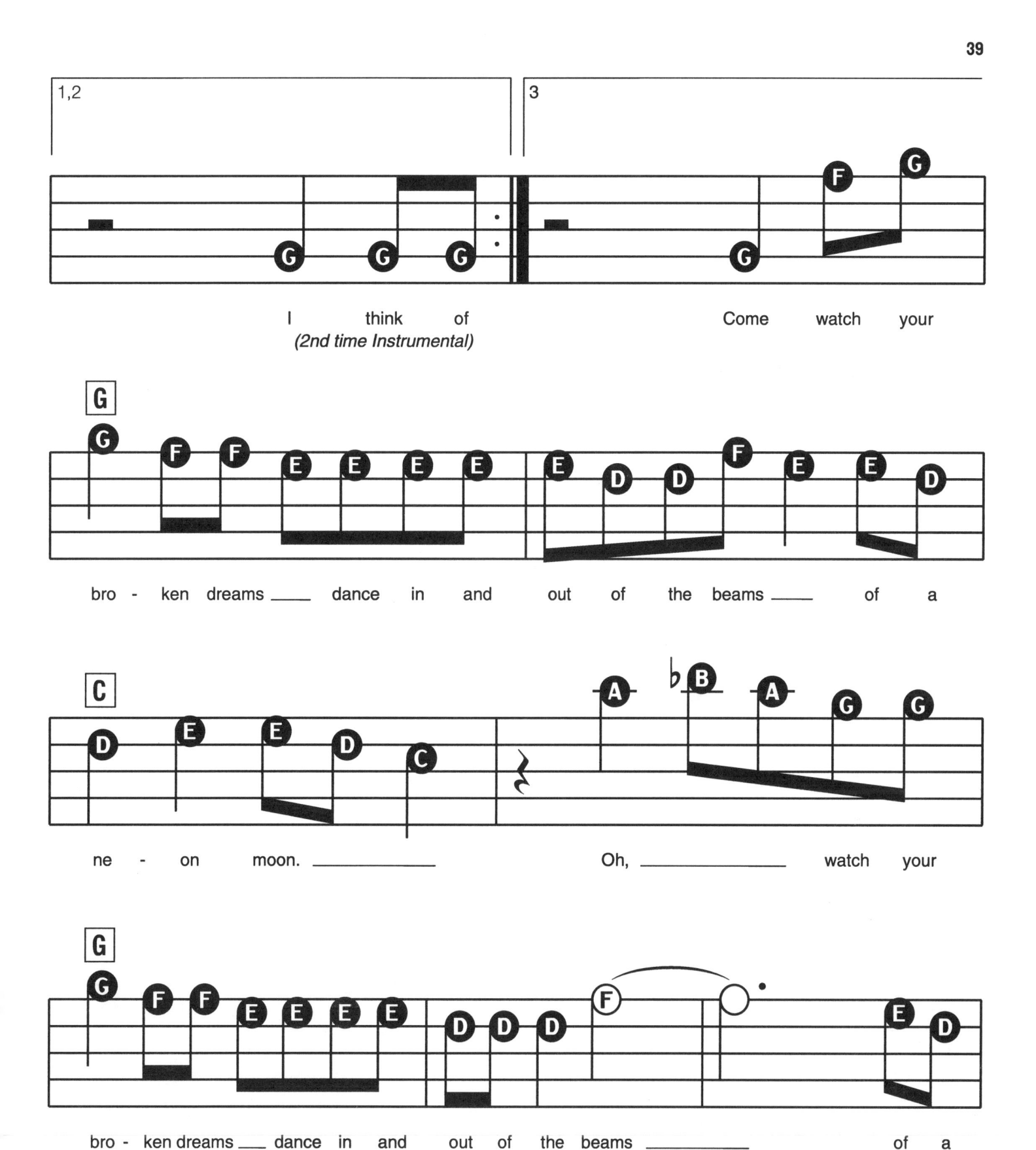

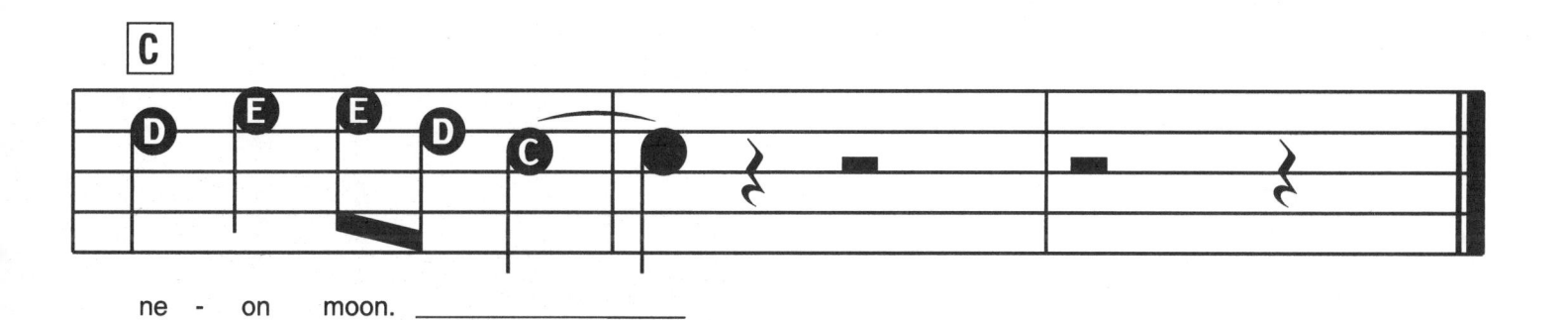

The River

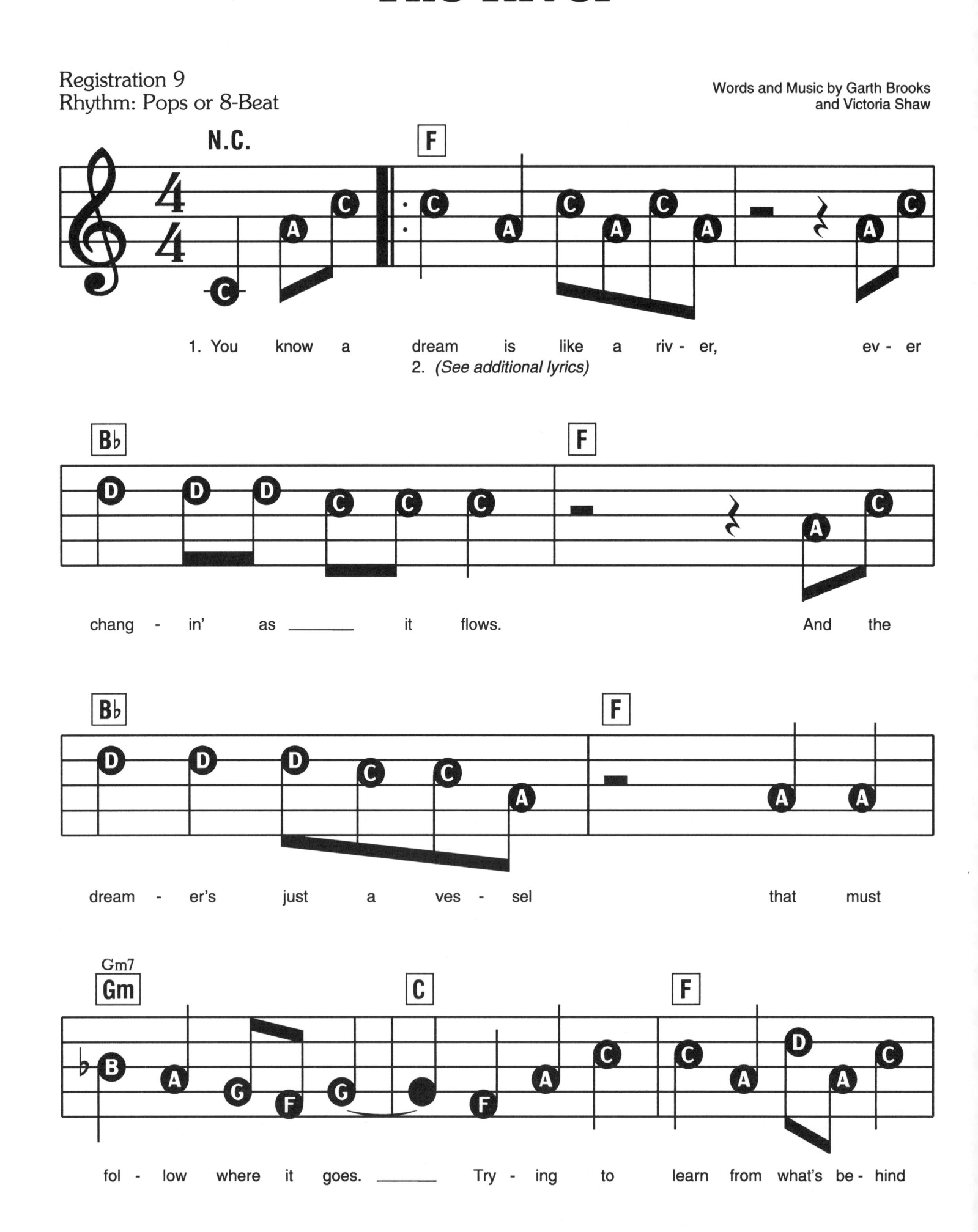

Registration 9
Rhythm: Pops or 8-Beat

Words and Music by Garth Brooks
and Victoria Shaw

1. You know a dream is like a riv- er, ev- er chang- in' as ____ it flows. And the dream- er's just a ves- sel that must fol- low where it goes. ____ Try- ing to learn from what's be- hind

2. *(See additional lyrics)*

Copyright © 1989 MAJOR BOB MUSIC CO., INC. (ASCAP), MID-SUMMER MUSIC CO., INC. (ASCAP) and GARY MORRIS MUSIC
International Copyright Secured   All Rights Reserved

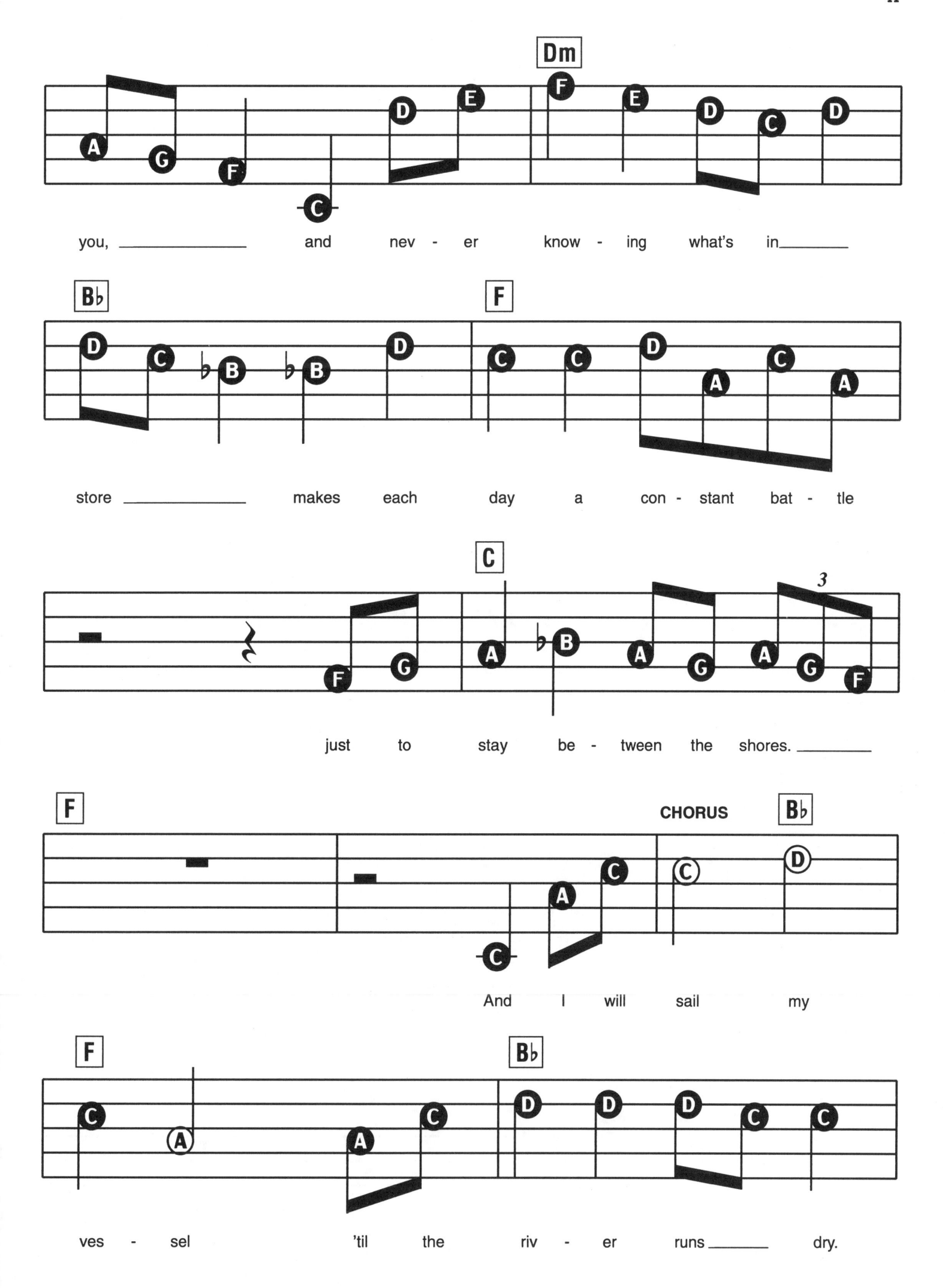

you, _____ and nev-er know-ing what's in _____ store _____ makes each day a con-stant bat-tle just to stay be-tween the shores. _____

CHORUS

And I will sail my ves-sel 'til the riv-er runs _____ dry.

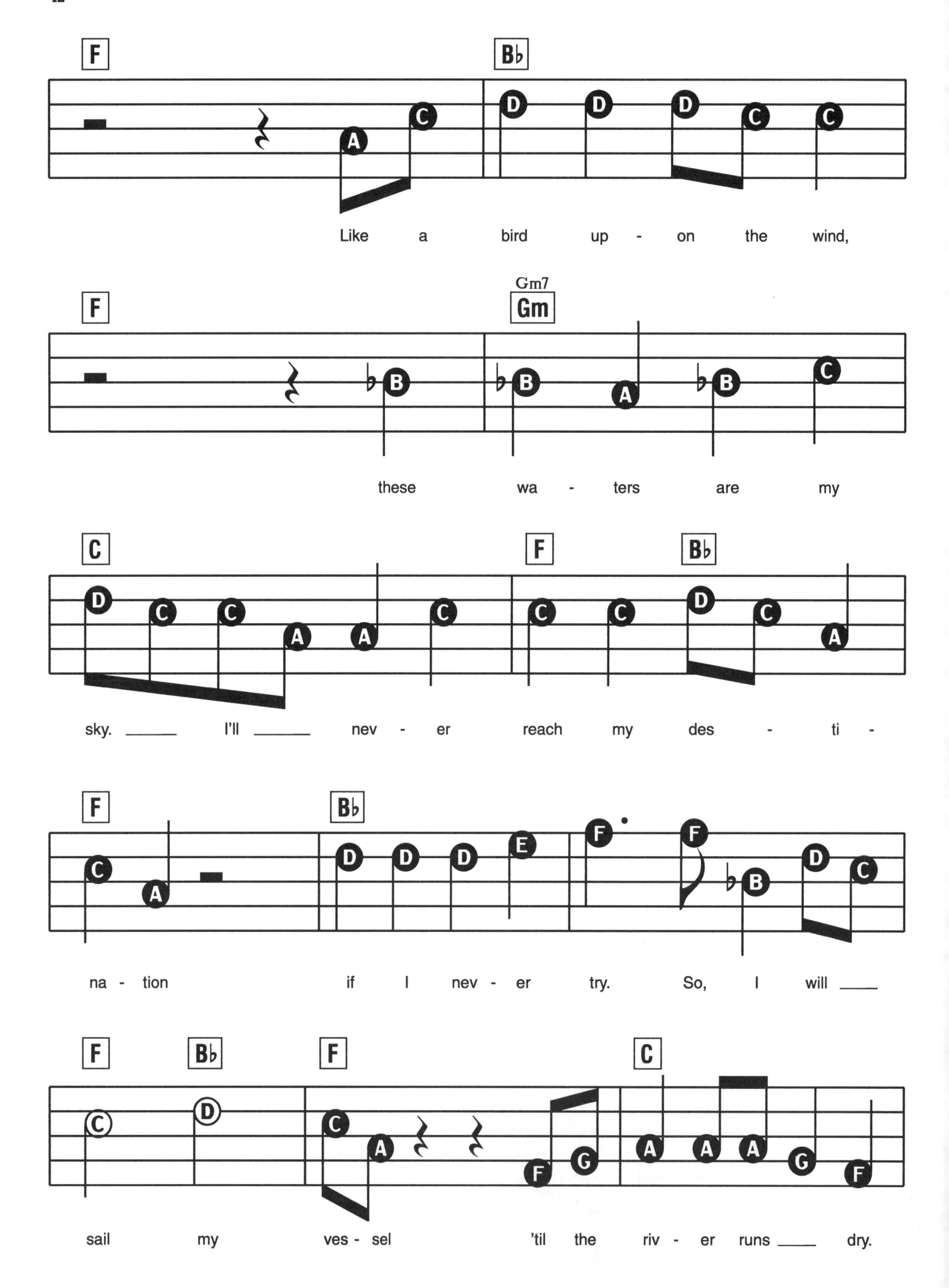

Like a bird up-on the wind, these wa-ters are my sky. I'll nev-er reach my des-ti-na-tion if I nev-er try. So, I will sail my ves-sel 'til the riv-er runs dry.

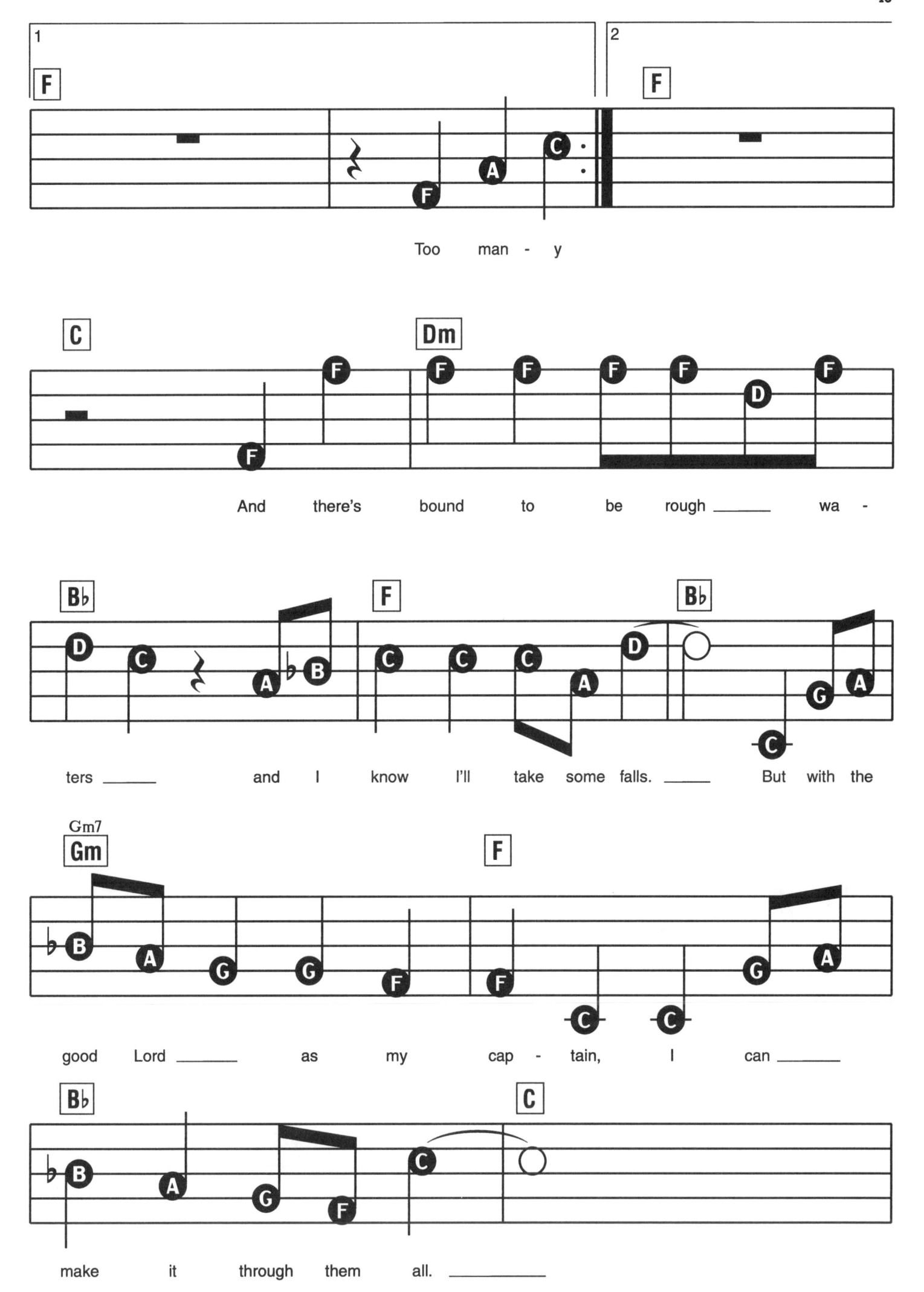

Too many / *And there's bound to be rough waters and I know I'll take some falls. But with the good Lord as my captain, I can make it through them all.*

CHORUS

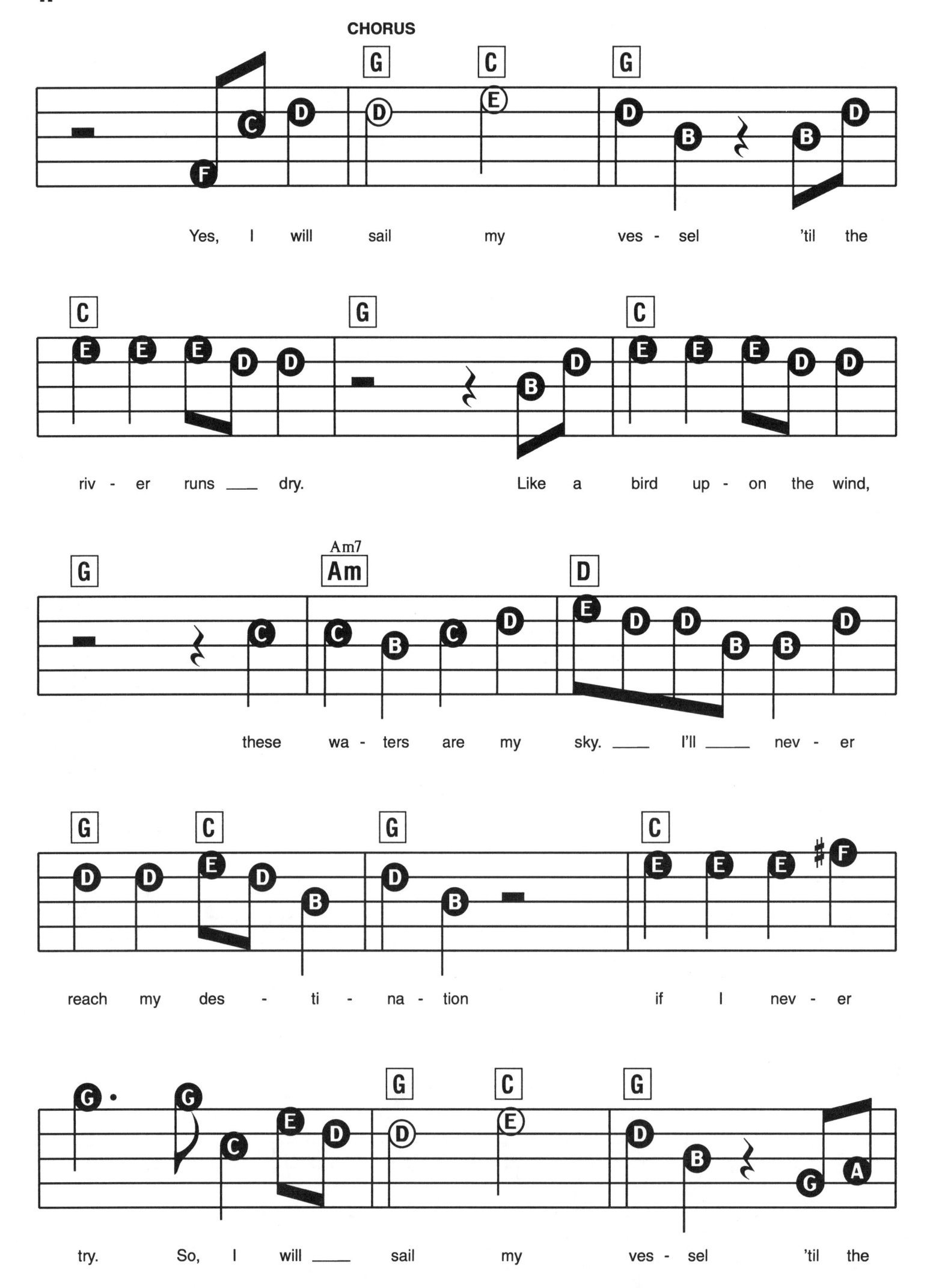

Yes, I will sail my ves-sel 'til the riv-er runs ___ dry. Like a bird up-on the wind, these wa-ters are my sky. ___ I'll ___ nev-er reach my des-ti-na-tion if I nev-er try. So, I will ___ sail my ves-sel 'til the riv - er runs ___ dry.   Yes, I will

sail   my   ves - sel   'til the   riv - er runs ___ dry.

'Til the

riv - er runs dry. ___

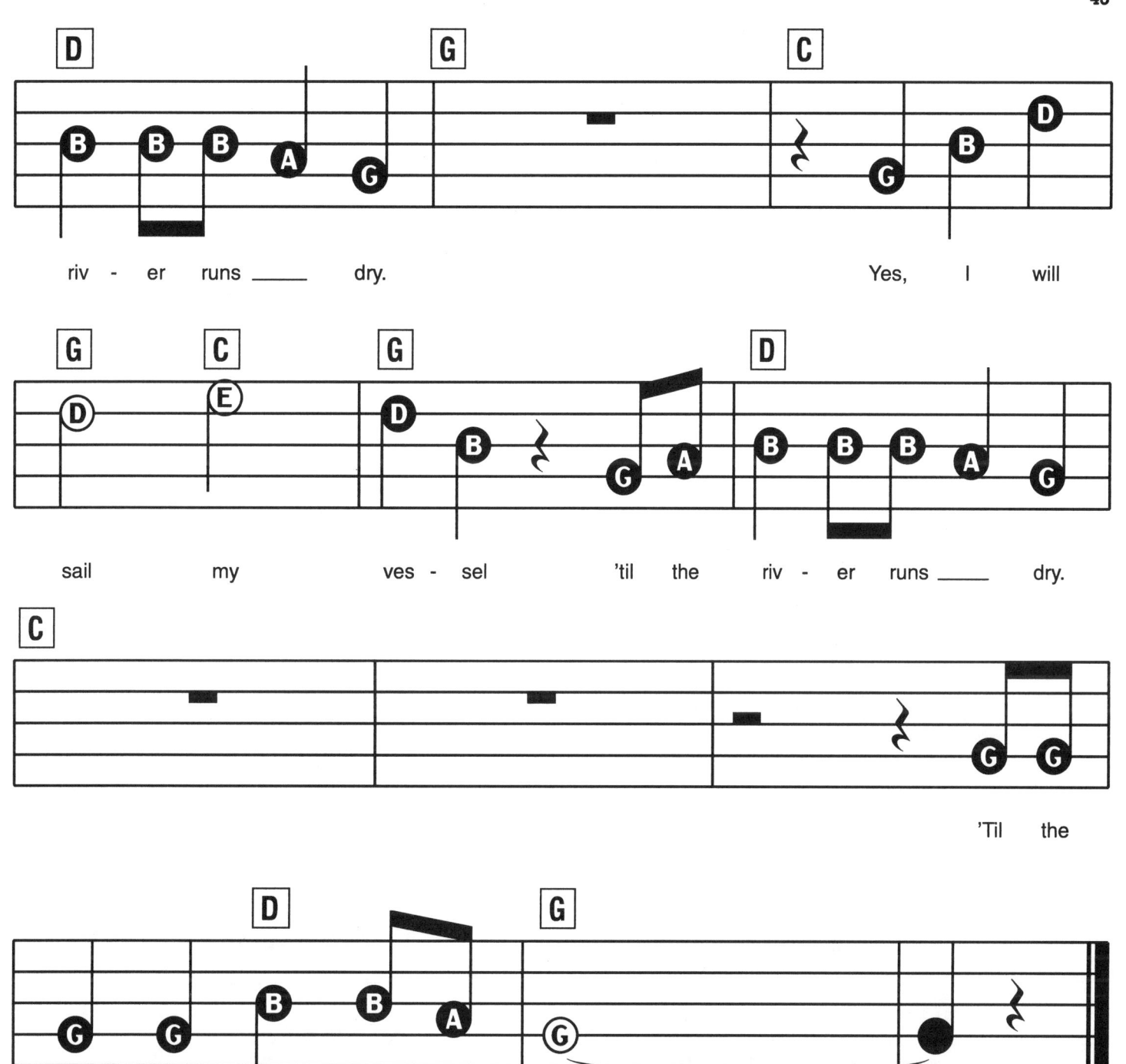

Additional Lyrics

2. Too many times we stand aside
   And let the waters slip away
   'Til what we put off 'til tomorrow
   Has now become today.
   So, don't you sit upon the shoreline
   And say you're satisfied.
   Choose to chance the rapids
   And dare to dance the tide. Yes, I will...
   To Chorus:

Sacred Ground

Registration 3
Rhythm: Pops or Country

Words and Music by Kix Brooks
and Vernon Rust

We got mar - ried in high school, had a
guess I took ____ for grant - ed she would

ba - by when we turned eight - een. ____
nev - er look at some - one else. ____ Now

I bagged gro - ceries in the day - time. ____ At
I got some patch - ing up to do. ____ Oh, and

night I learned to fix T. V.'s. ____ When you
I don't need your help. ____

Copyright © 1987 Cross Keys Publishing Co., Inc. and David 'N' Will Music
All Rights on behalf of Cross Keys Publishing Co., Inc. administered by Sony Music Publishing,
8 Music Square West, Nashville, TN 37203
International Copyright Secured   All Rights Reserved

47

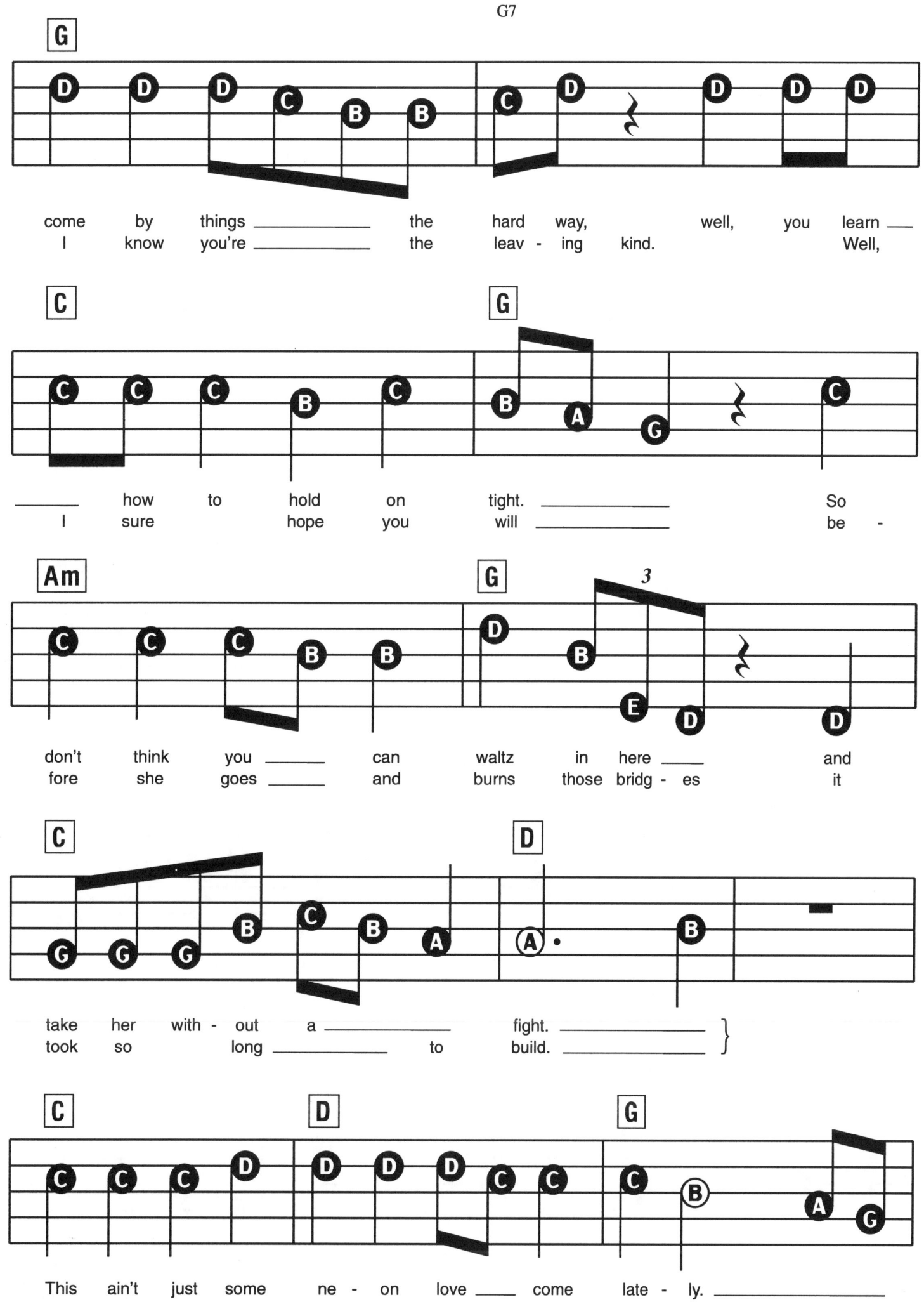

[G] [G7]

come by things _____ the hard way, well, you learn _____
I know you're _____ the leav-ing kind. Well,

[C] [G]

_____ how to hold on tight. _____ So
I sure hope on you will _____ be-

[Am] [G]

don't think you _____ can waltz in here _____ and
fore she goes _____ and burns those bridg-es it

[C] [D]

take her with-out a _____ fight. _____
took so long _____ to build. _____

[C] [D] [G]

This ain't just some ne-on love _____ come late-ly. _____

It's a pre-cious thing ___ you don't know noth-ing a-bout. ___ We were joined ___ in the eyes of the Lord, in the eyes of our home-town. Why don't you leave her a-lone? You're tread-ing on sa-cred ground. ___

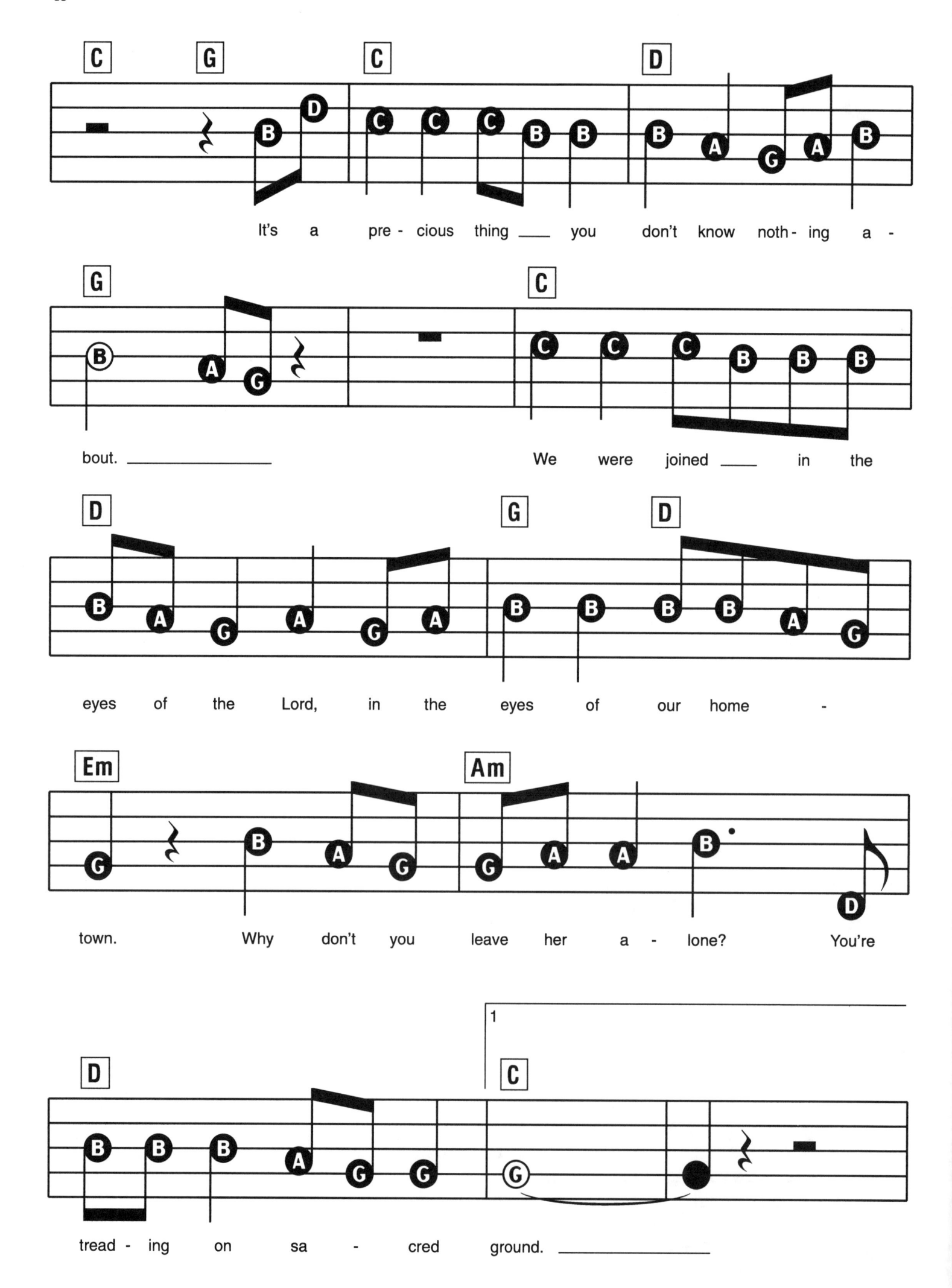

I ground. Go on and leave her a-lone. Why don't you leave her a-lone? Go on and leave her a-lone. You're tread-ing on sa-cred ground.

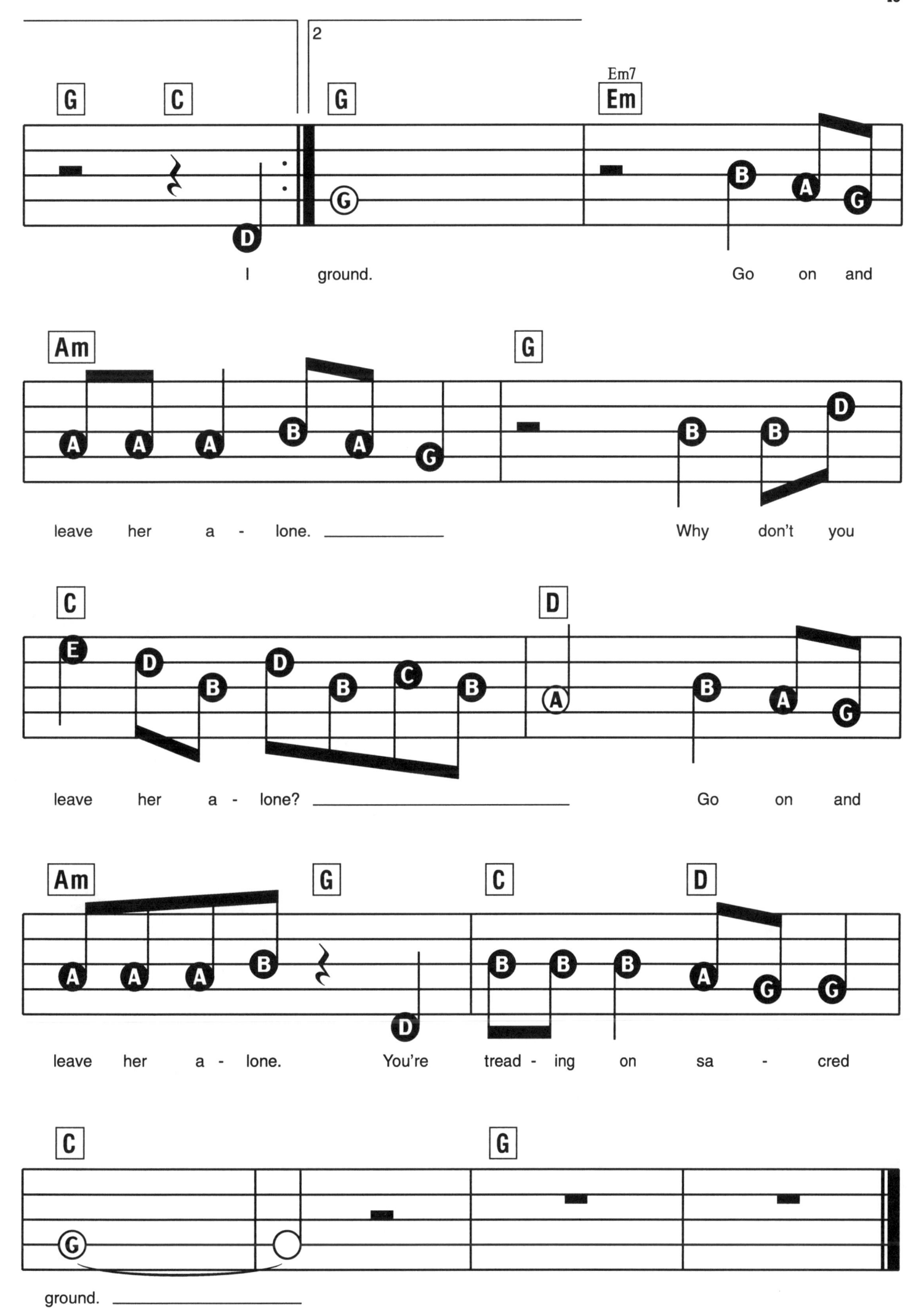

She Is His Only Need

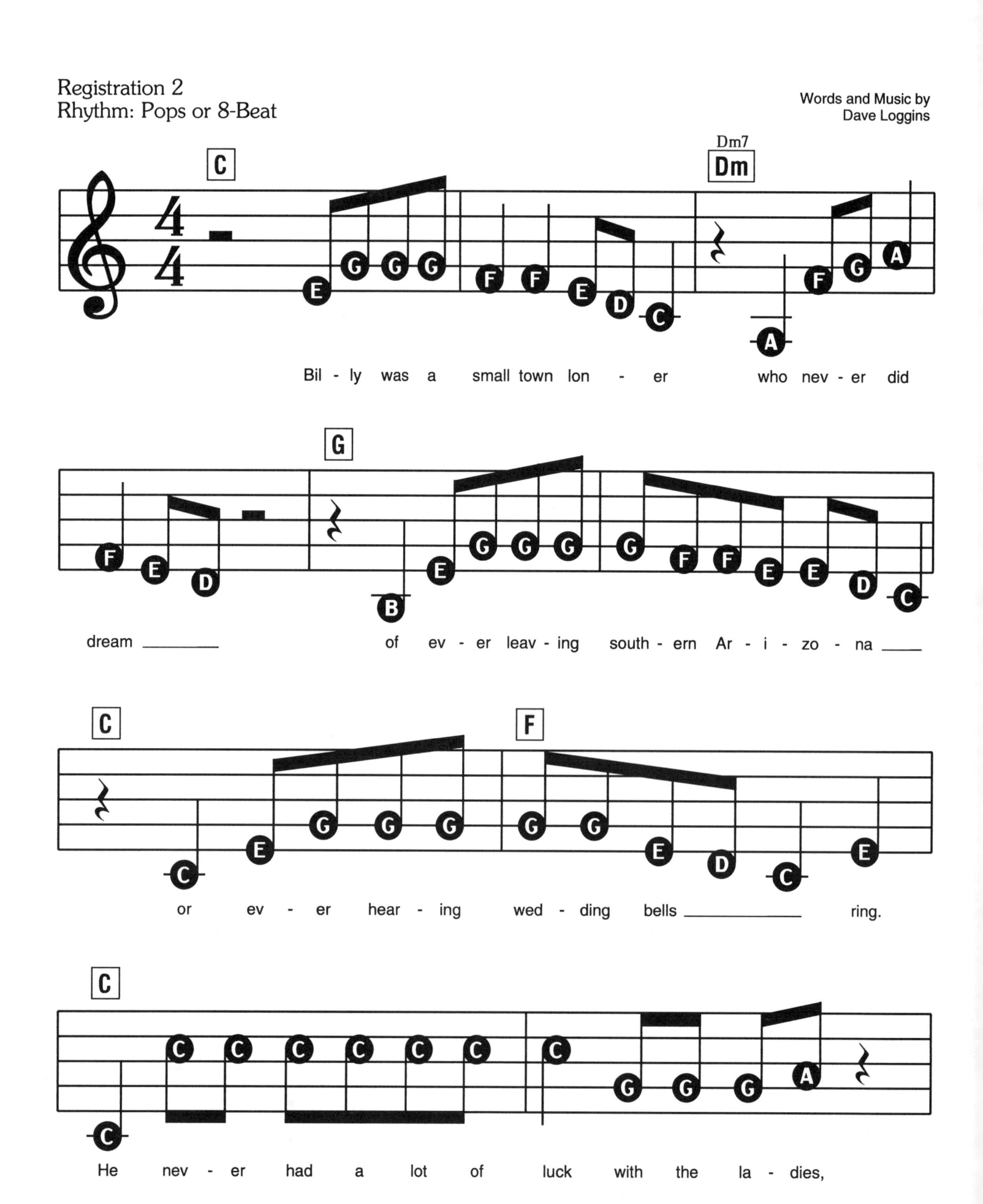

Registration 2
Rhythm: Pops or 8-Beat

Words and Music by
Dave Loggins

Bil - ly was a small town lon - er who nev - er did dream _____ of ev - er leav - ing south - ern Ar - i - zo - na _____ or ev - er hear - ing wed - ding bells _____ ring. He nev - er had a lot of luck with the la - dies,

© Copyright 1992 by MCA MUSIC PUBLISHING, A Division of MCA INC. and EMERALD RIVER MUSIC
Sole Selling Agent MCA MUSIC PUBLISHING, A Division of MCA INC., 1755 Broadway, New York, NY 10019
International Copyright Secured   All Rights Reserved
MCA music publishing

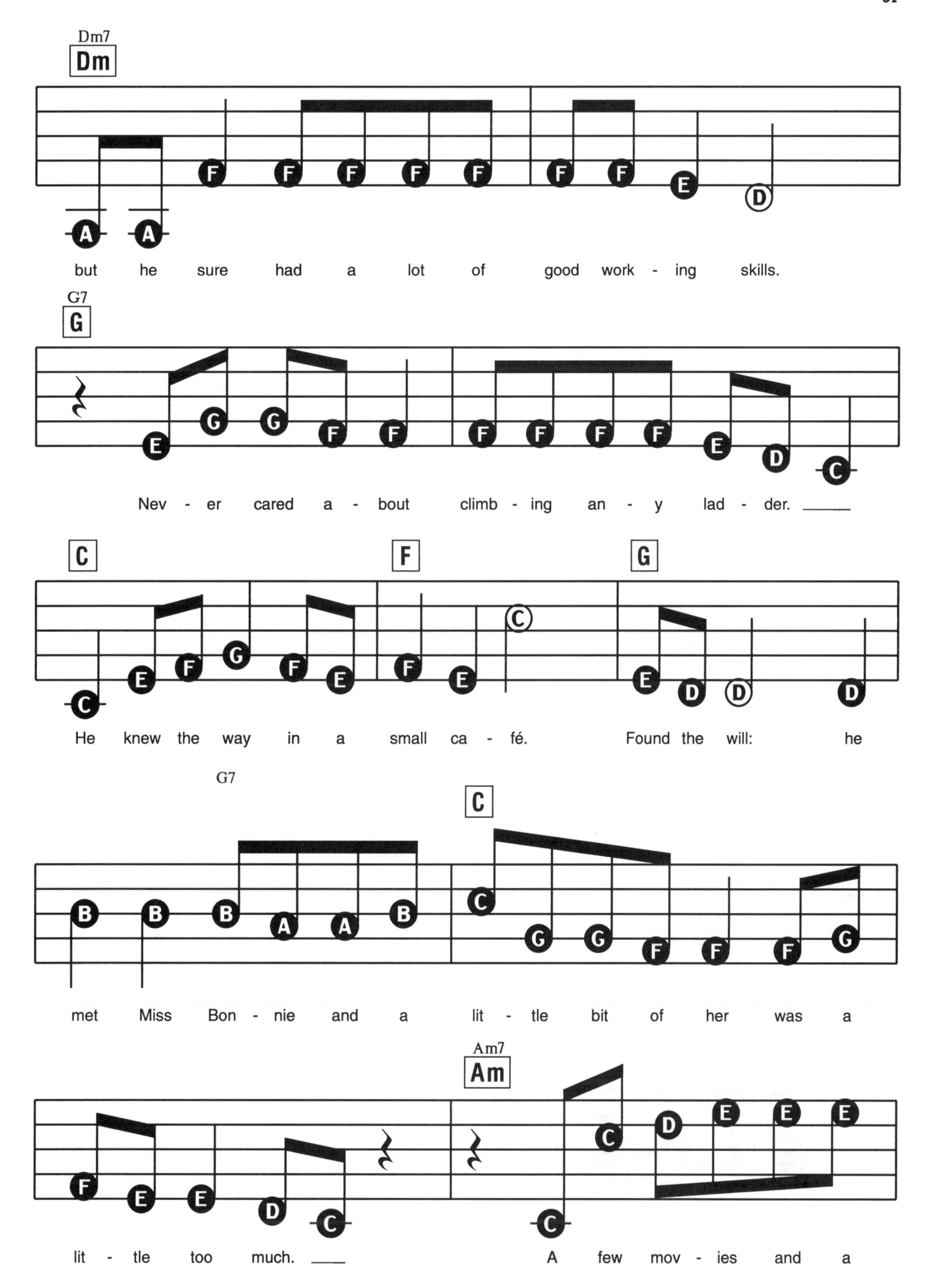

but he sure had a lot of good working skills.
Never cared about climbing any ladder.
He knew the way in a small café. Found the will: he
met Miss Bonnie and a little bit of her was a
little too much. A few movies and a

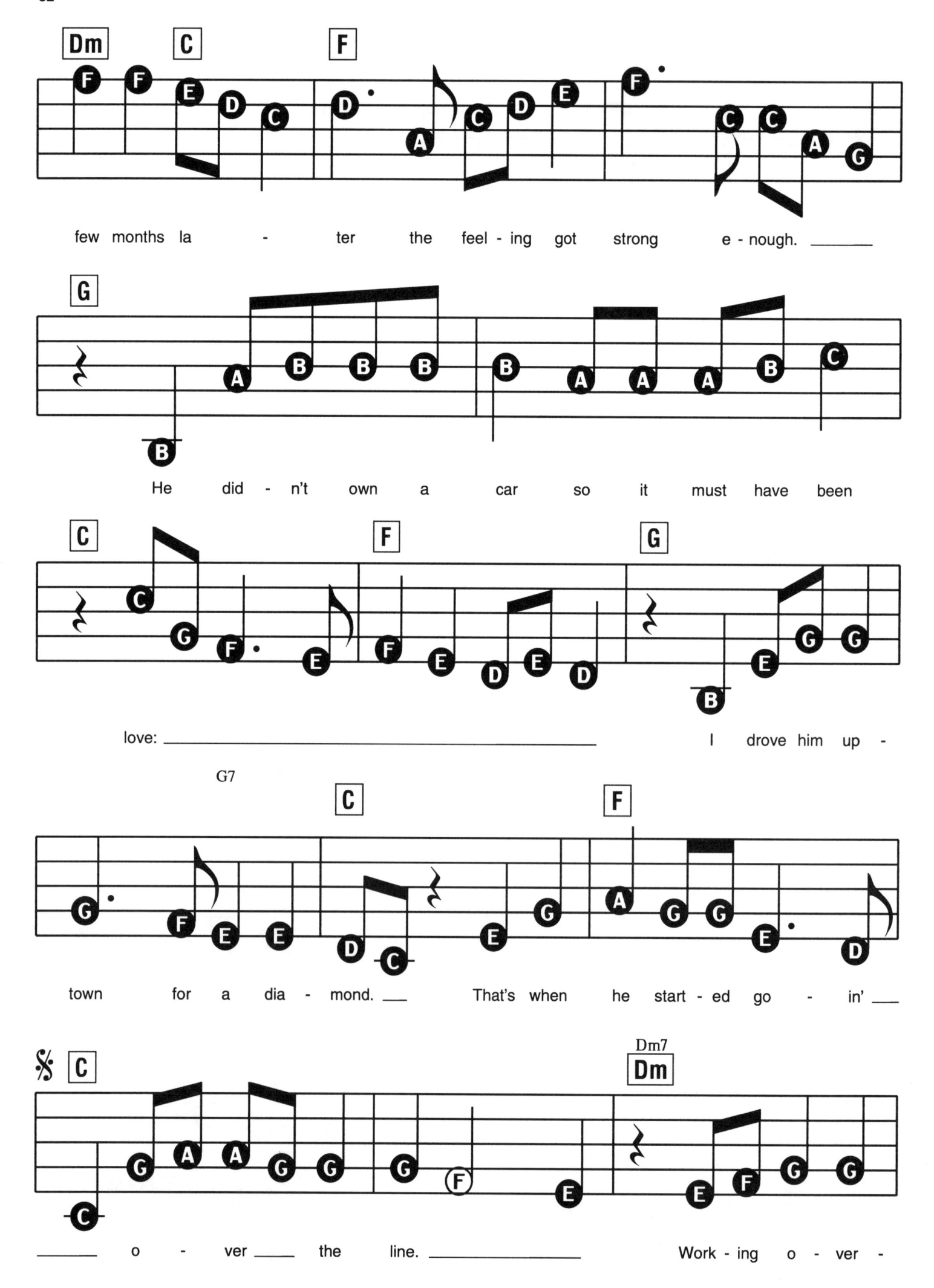

few months la - ter the feel - ing got strong e - nough. He did - n't own a car so it must have been love: I drove him up - town for a dia - mond. That's when he start - ed go - in' o - ver the line. Work - ing o - ver -

time ____ to give her things just to hear her say she don't ___ de - serve 'em. But he loved her and he just kept go - in' ___ o - ver - board, _____ o - ver the lim - it to af - ford ____ to give her things he knew she want - ed. 'Cause with - out her where ____ would he ____

be? ____ See, it's not for him. ____

She is his on - ly ____ need. ____

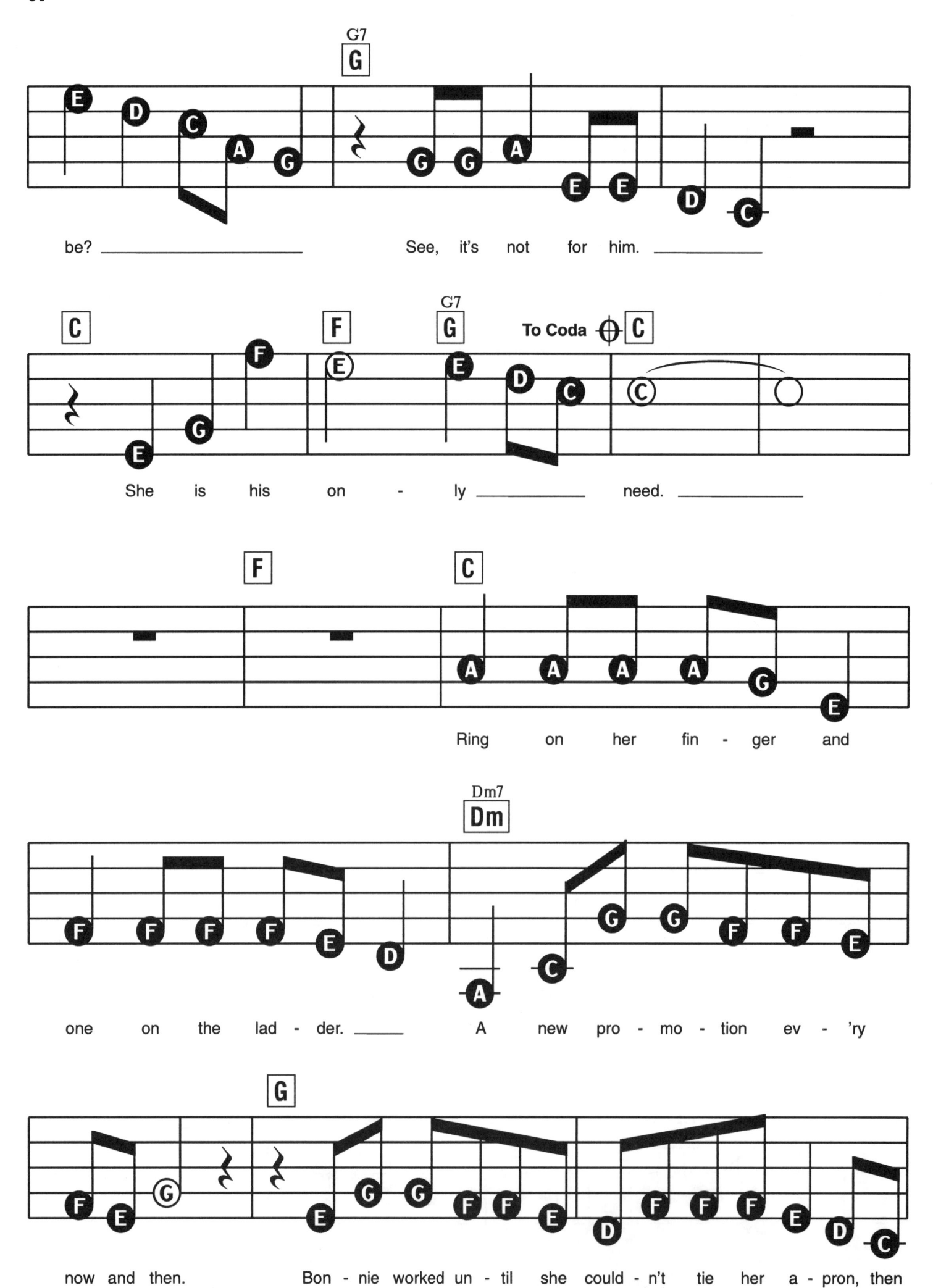

Ring on her fin - ger and

one on the lad - der. ____ A new pro - mo - tion ev - 'ry

now and then. Bon - nie worked un - til she could - n't tie her a - pron, then

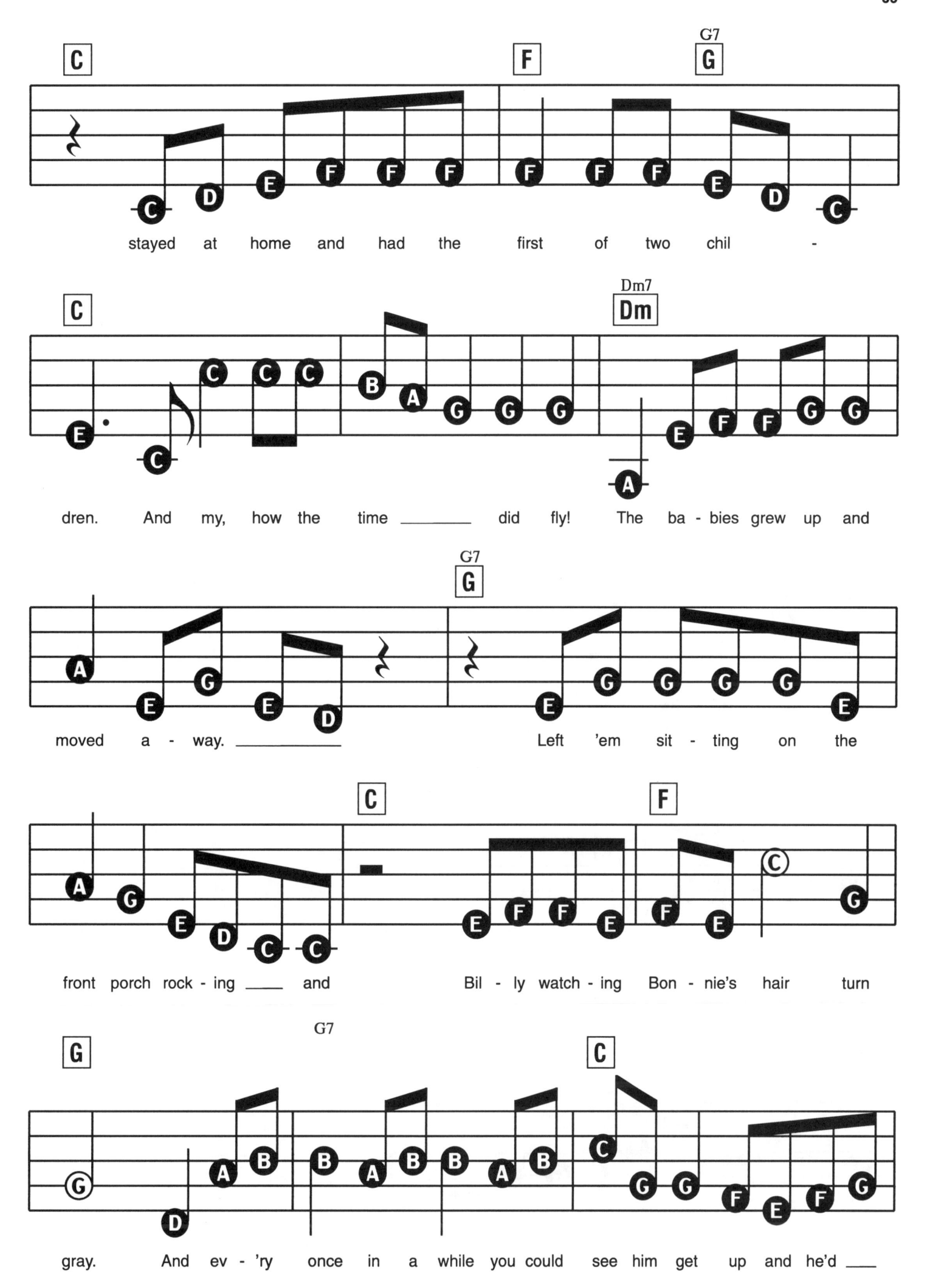

stayed at home and had the first of two chil-
dren. And my, how the time ____ did fly! The babies grew up and
moved a-way. ____ Left 'em sit-ting on the
front porch rock-ing ____ and Bil-ly watch-ing Bon-nie's hair turn
gray. And ev-'ry once in a while you could see him get up and he'd ____

56

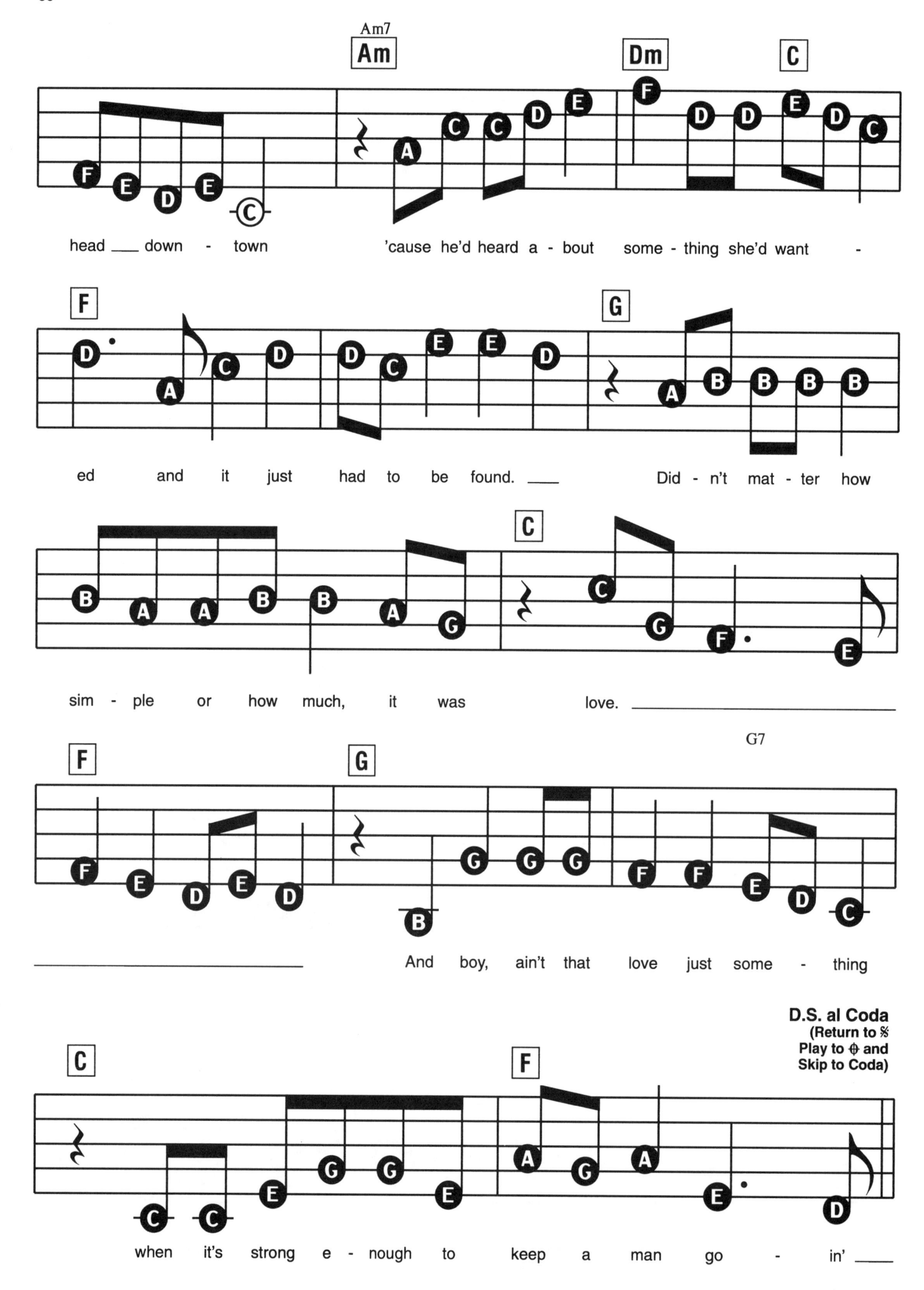

head __ down - town   'cause he'd heard a - bout some - thing she'd want - ed and it just had to be found. __ Did - n't mat - ter how sim - ple or how much, it was love. __ And boy, ain't that love just some - thing when it's strong e - nough to keep a man go - in' __

D.S. al Coda
(Return to 𝄋
Play to ⊕ and
Skip to Coda)

57

need.
(O - ver the line, ____ work - ing o - ver -
(Instrumental on repeat)

time. She is his on - ly His on - ly ____

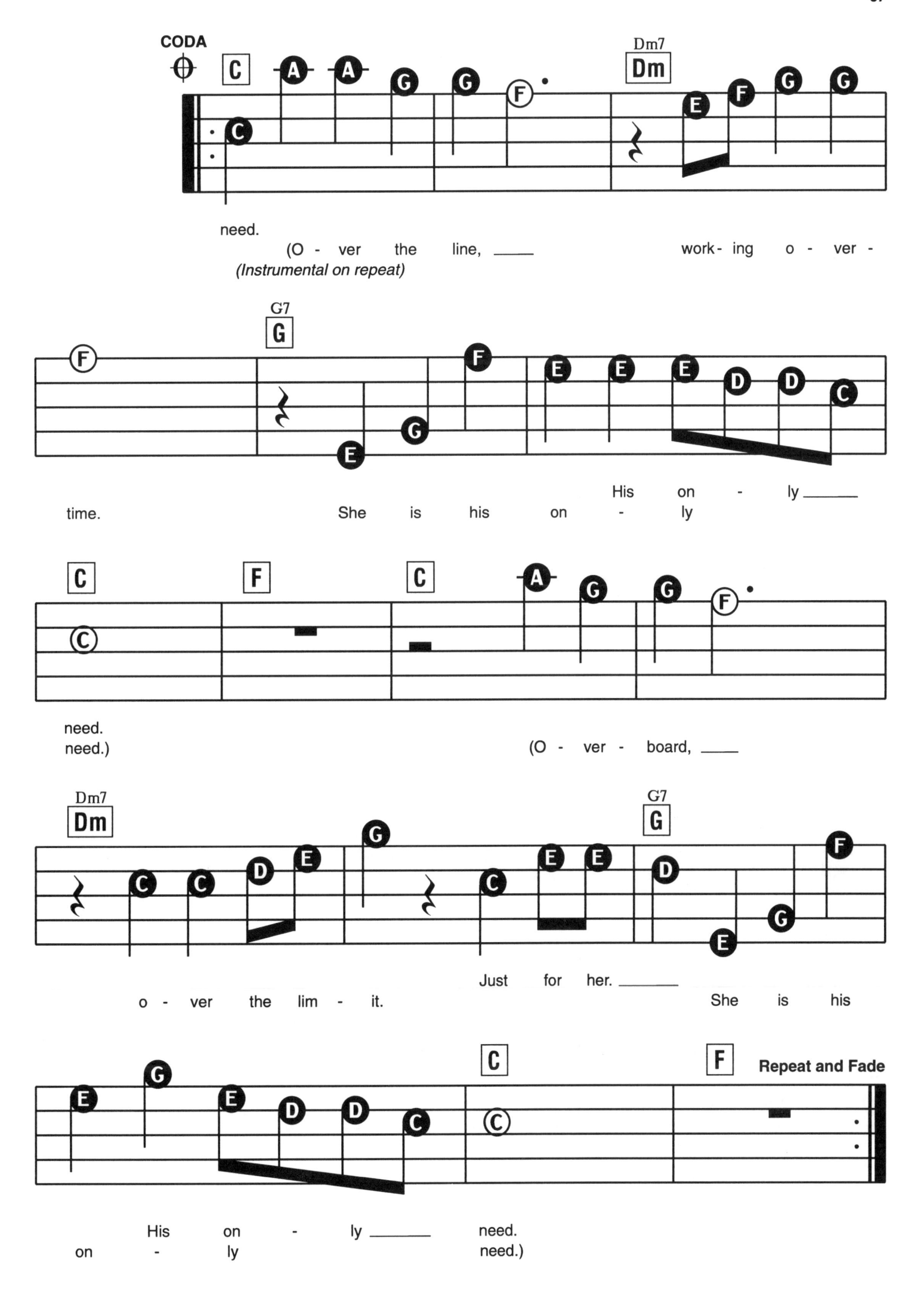

need.
need.) (O - ver - board, ____

o - ver the lim - it. Just for her. ____ She is his

Repeat and Fade

His on - ly ____ need.
on - ly need.)

Take A Little Trip

Registration 1
Rhythm: Rock or 8-Beat

Words and Music by Ronnie Rogers
and Mark Wright

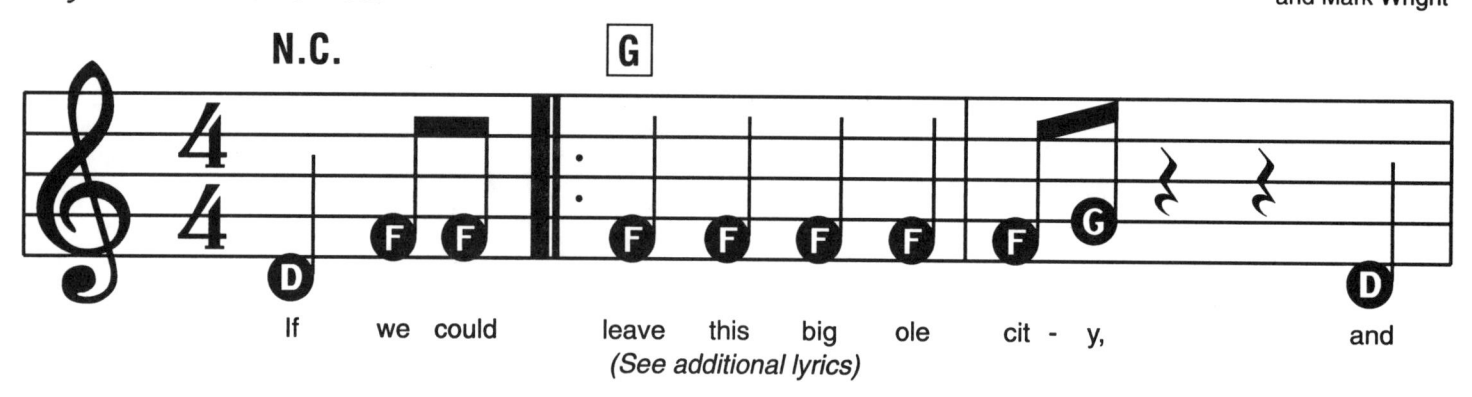

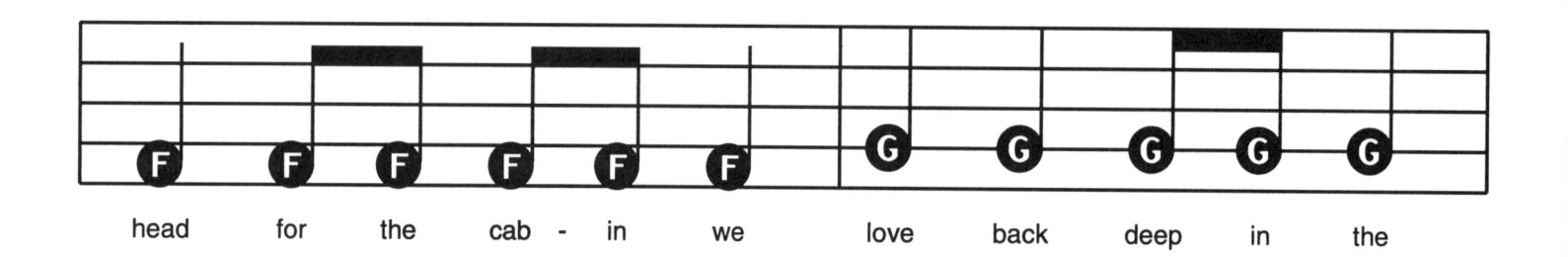

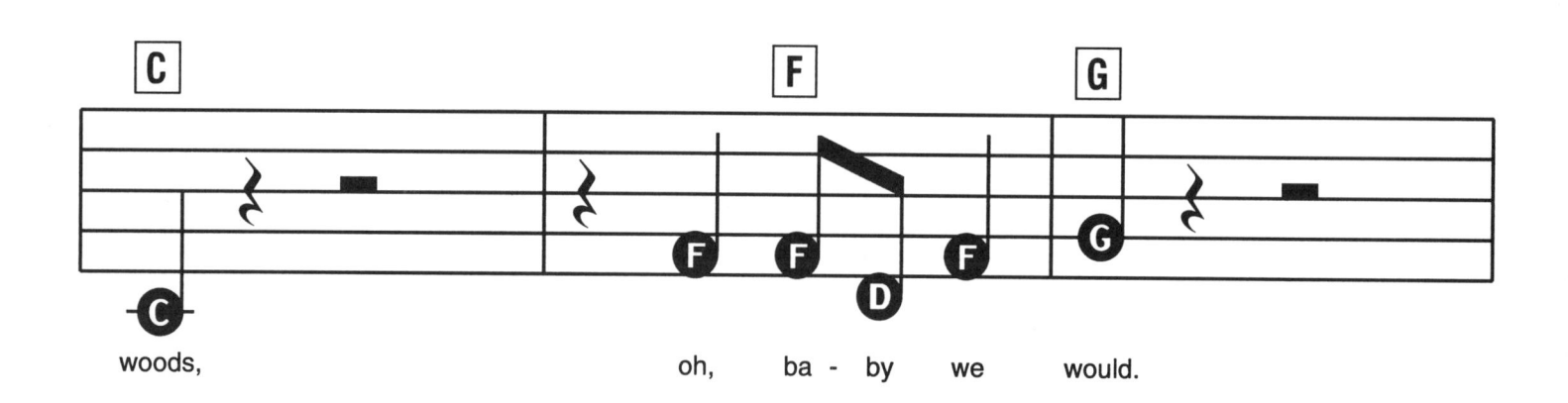

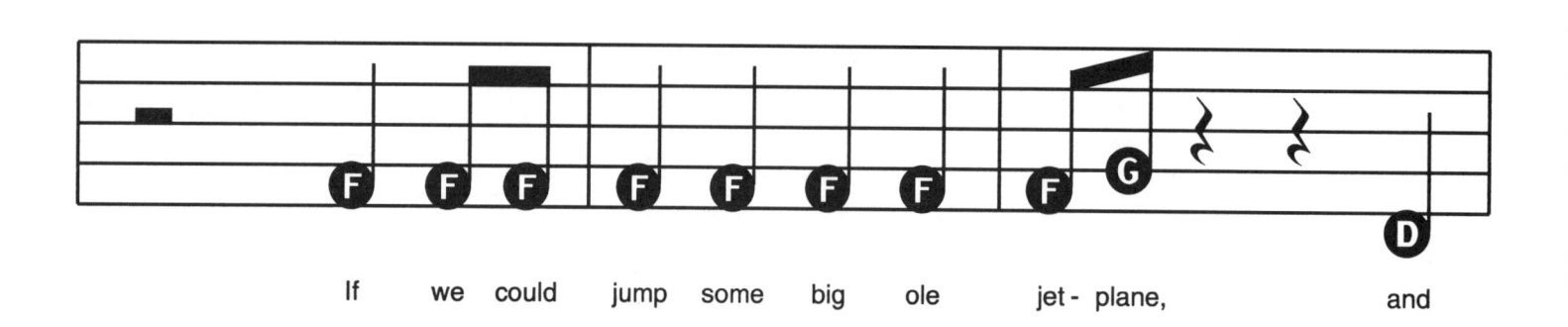

If we could leave this big ole cit-y,
(See additional lyrics)
and head for the cab-in we love back deep in the woods, oh, ba-by we would.

If we could jump some big ole jet-plane, and

© 1992 MAYPOP MUSIC (a division of Wildcountry, Inc.) EMI BLACKWOOD MUSIC INC. and WRIGHTCHILD MUSIC
Rights on behalf of WRIGHTCHILD MUSIC controlled and administered by EMI BLACKWOOD MUSIC INC.
All Rights Reserved

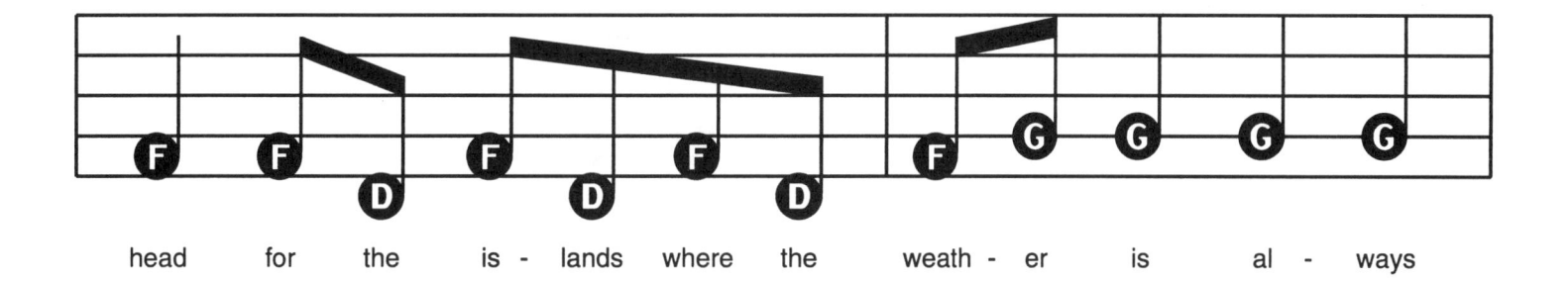

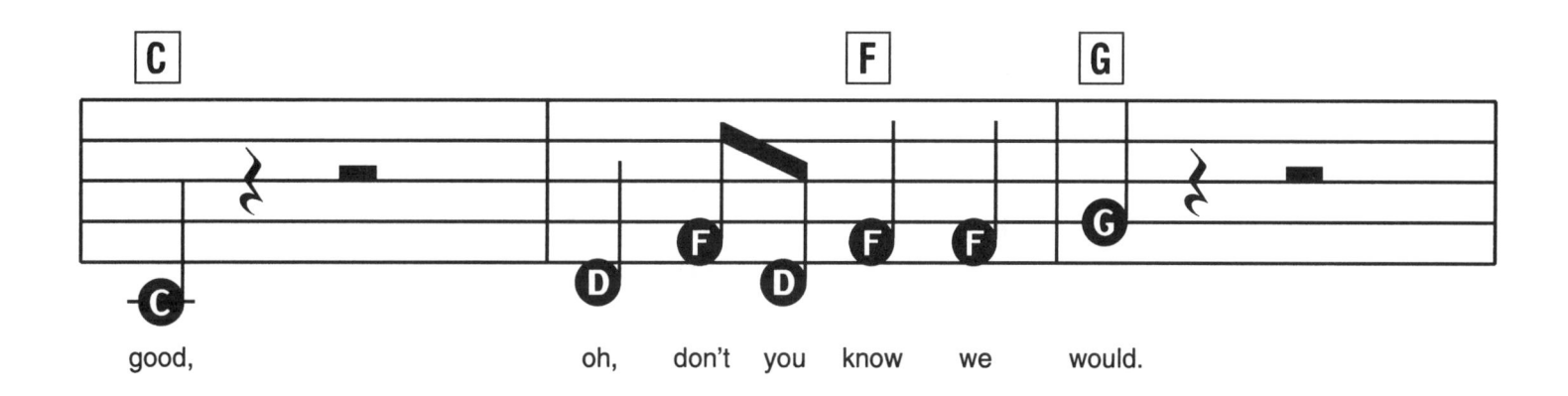

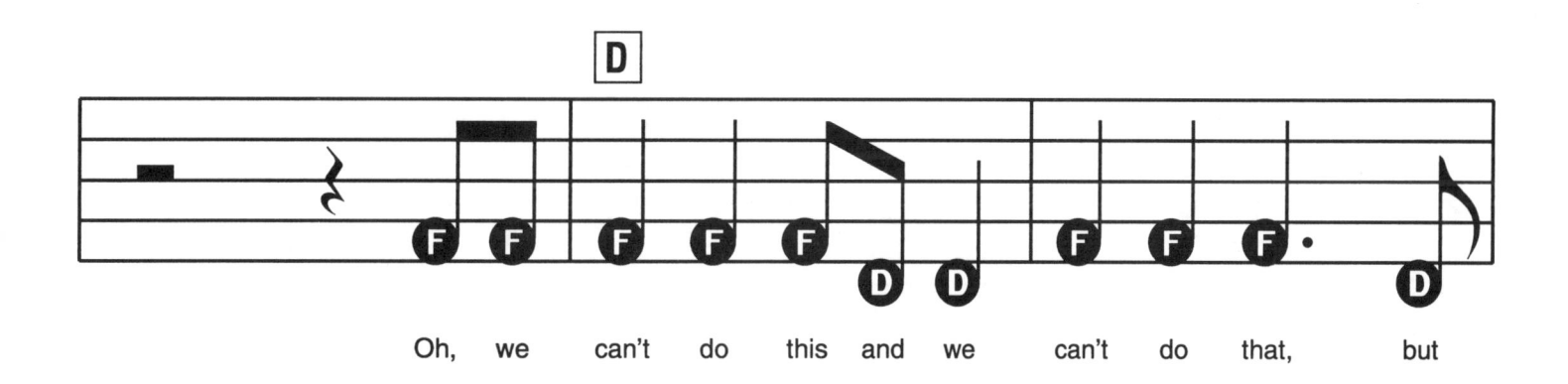

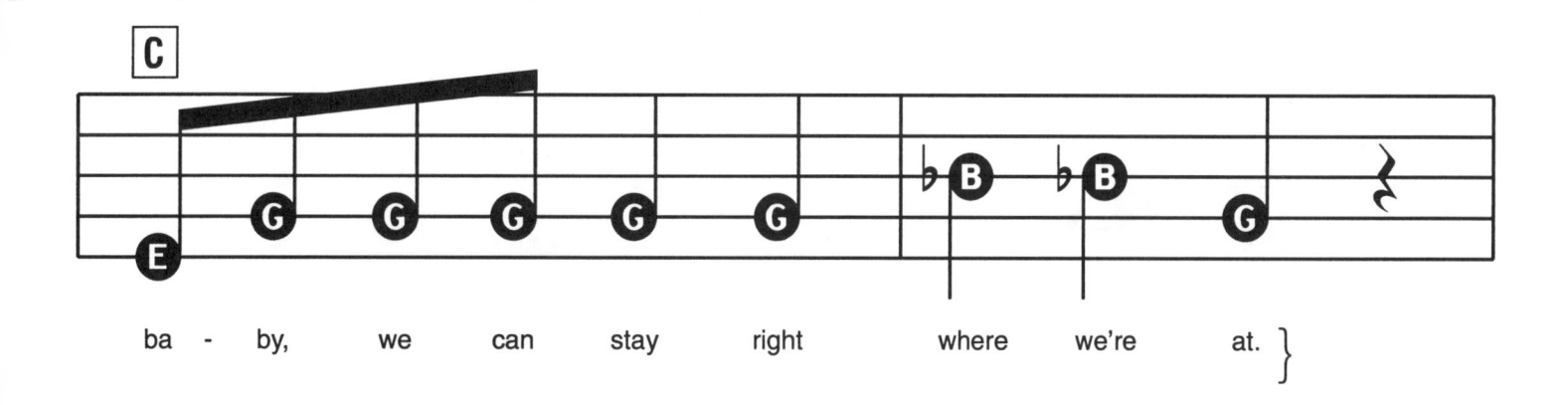

head for the is - lands where the weath - er is al - ways

good, oh, don't you know we would.

Oh, we can't do this and we can't do that, but

ba - by, we can stay right where we're at.

CHORUS

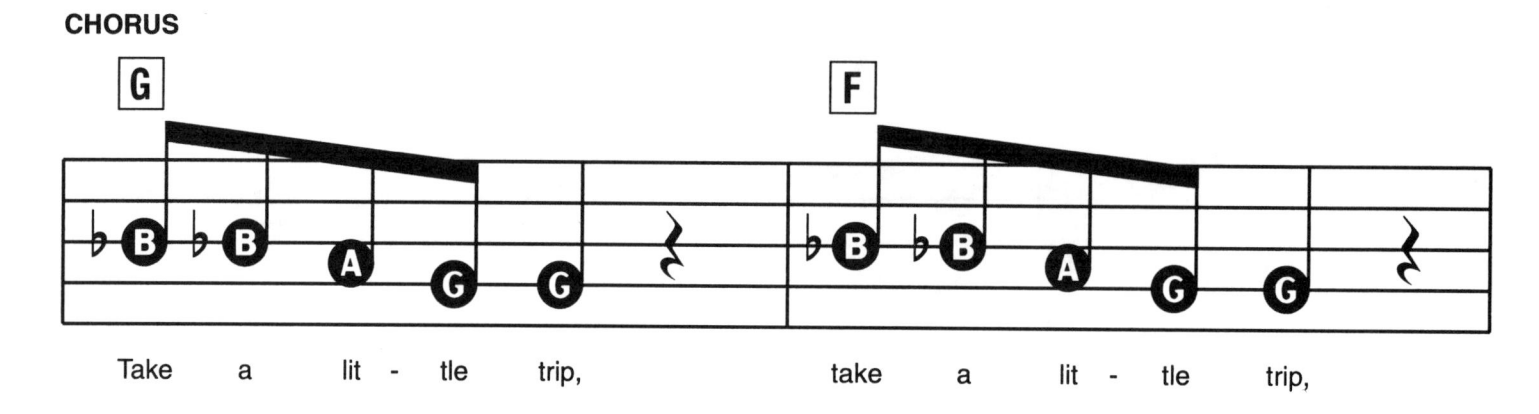

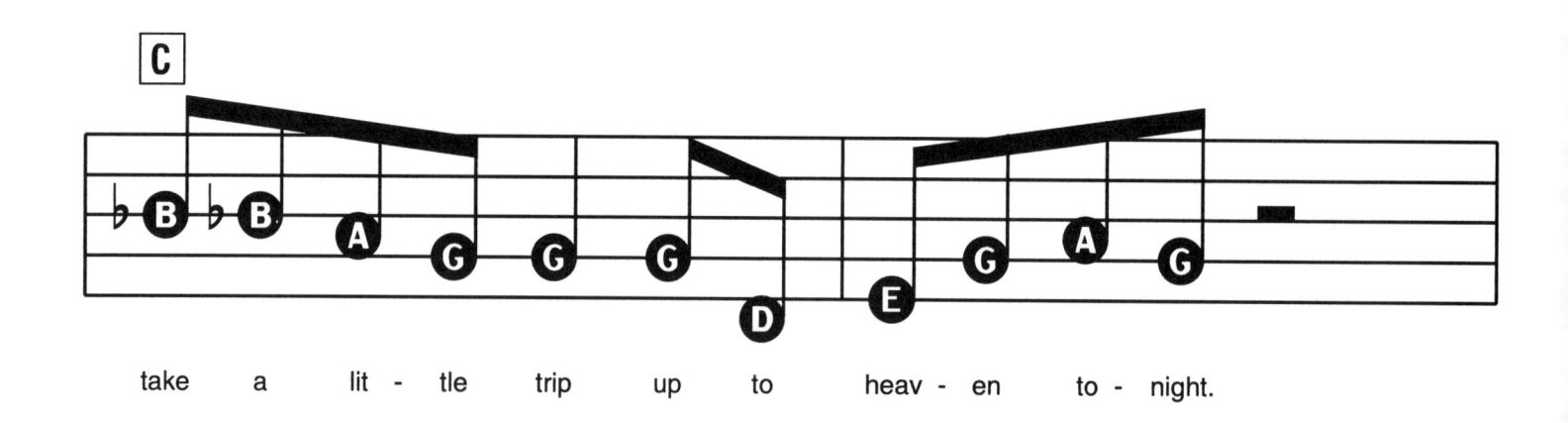

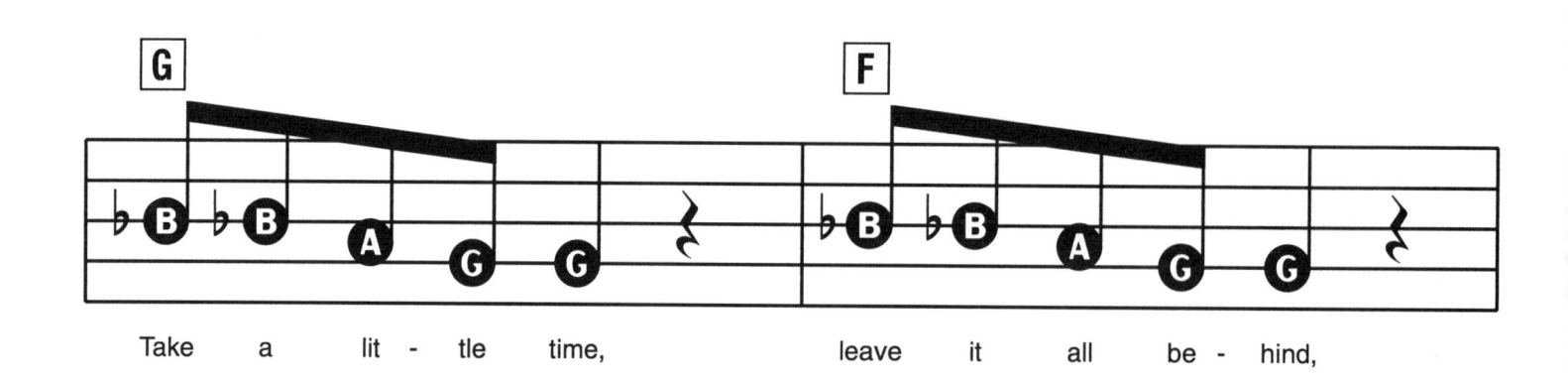

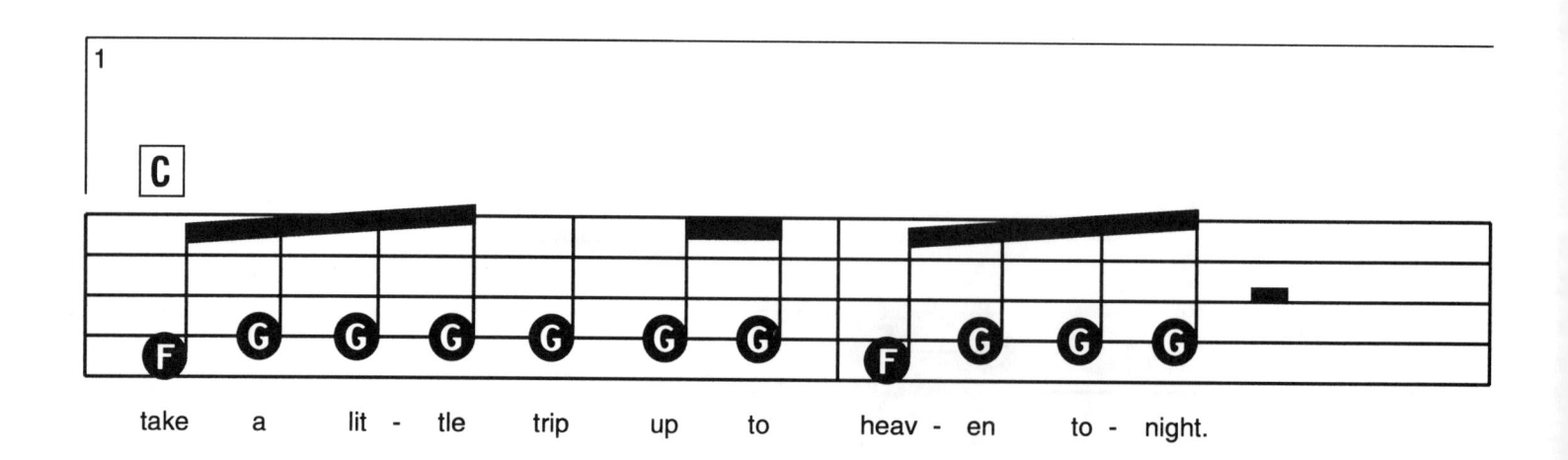

G Take a lit-tle trip, **F** take a lit-tle trip,

C take a lit-tle trip up to heav-en to-night.

G Take a lit-tle time, **F** leave it all be-hind,

1.
C take a lit-tle trip up to heav-en to-night.

2
G
C
We can take a lit - tle trip, you and
me out of sight.
D
Pull down the shades,
Em
C
turn out the lights,
take a lit - tle trip up to
heav - en to - night.
3
G
F
Take a lit - tle trip,
take a lit - tle trip,

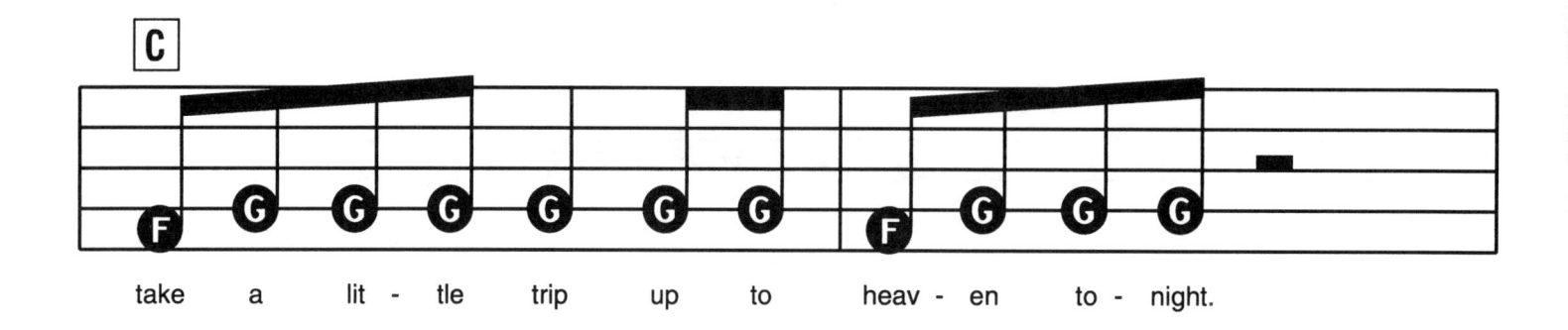

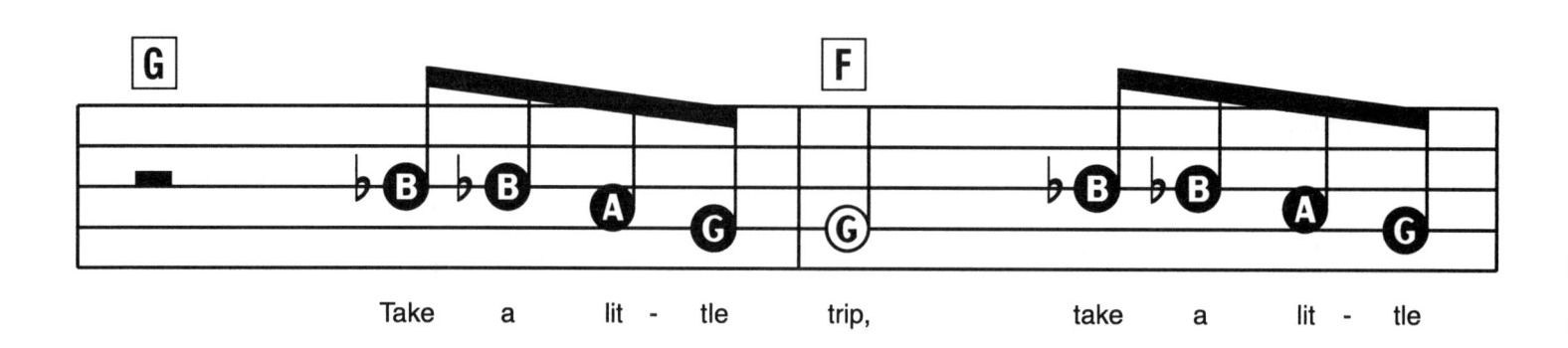

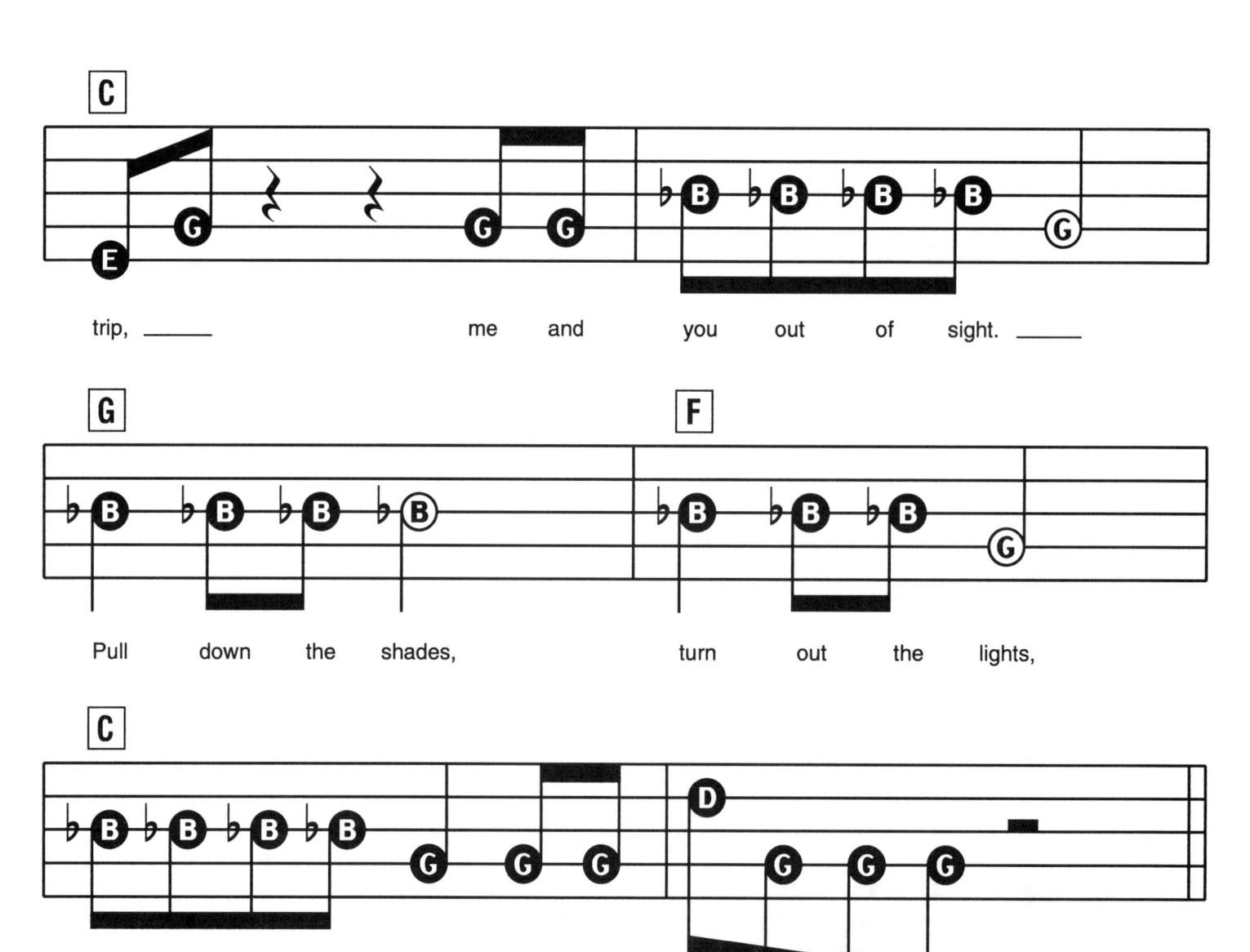

take a lit-tle trip up to heav-en to-night.

Take a lit-tle trip, take a lit-tle

trip, _____ me and you out of sight. _____

Pull down the shades, turn out the lights,

take a lit-tle trip up to heav-en to-night.

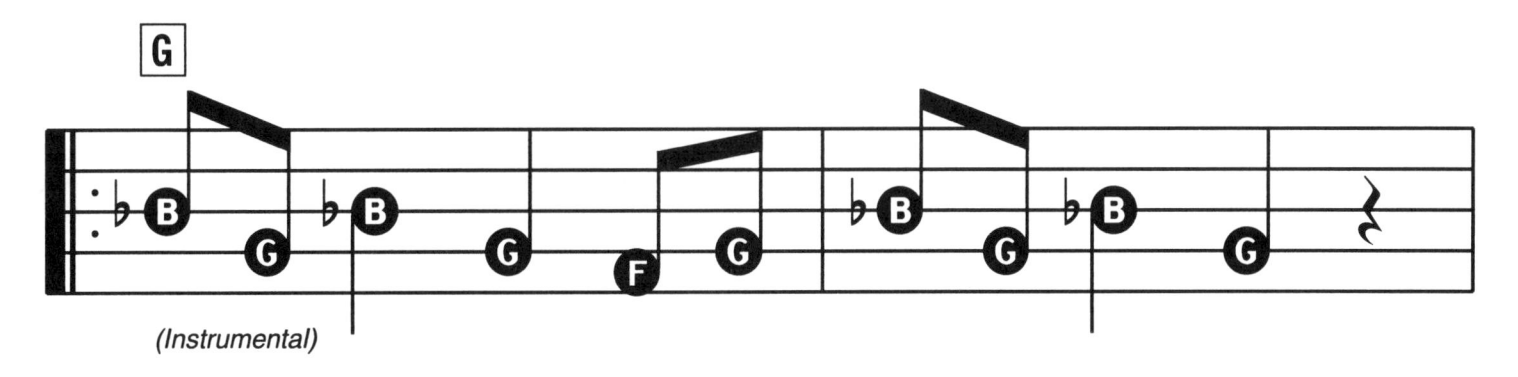

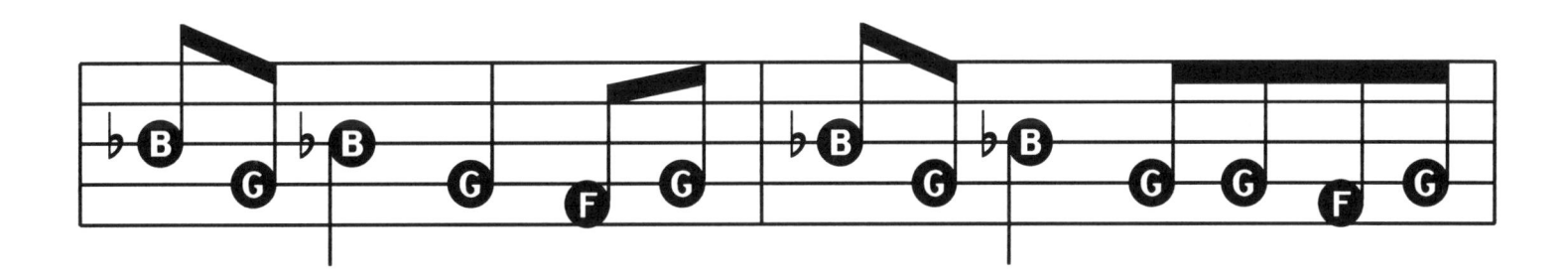

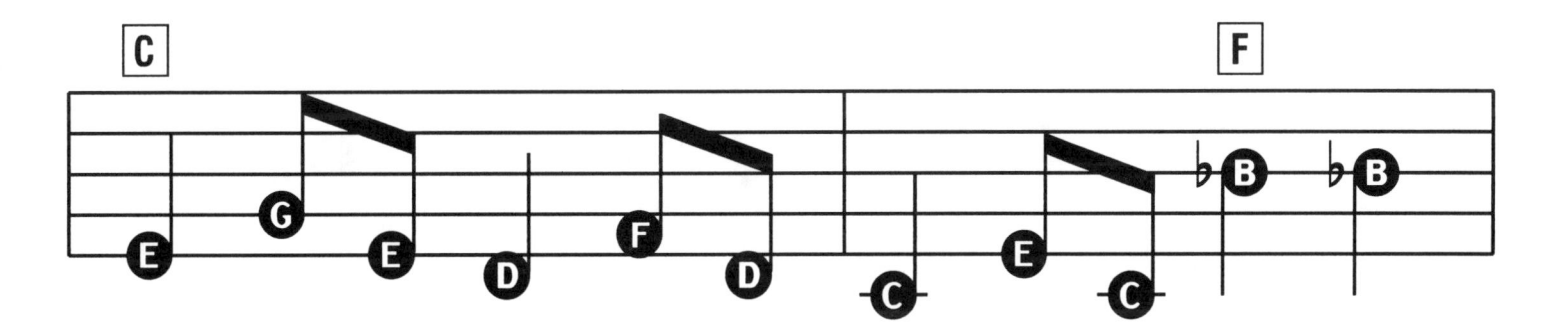

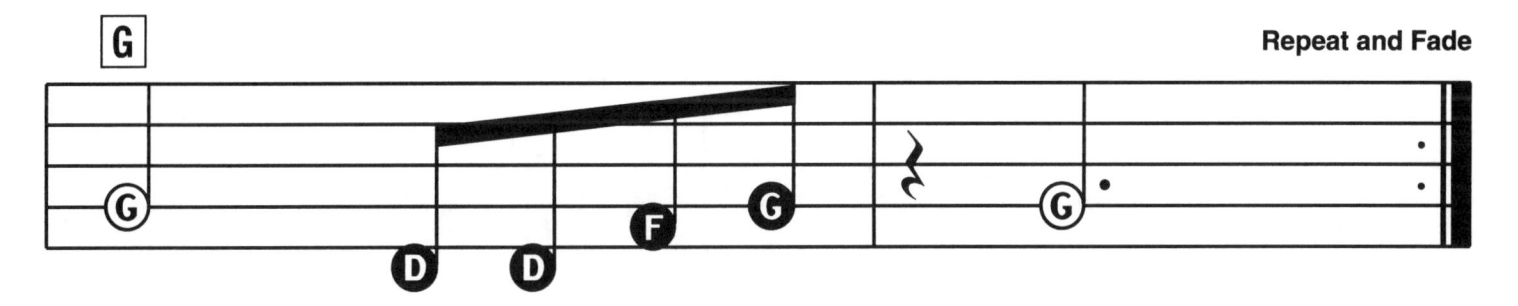

Additional Lyrics

We can go downtown to a night club,
Dance to the rhythm of the music
    on that old hardwood,
Oh, baby, we could.
Or we can call up Rita and Bobby,
And see what they're doin' tonight,
And maybe play some rook,
Oh, baby, we could.

Yeah, now we can do this, or we can do that,
Or baby, we can stay right where we're at.
To Chorus:

There Ain't Nothin' Wrong With The Radio

Registration 8
Rhythm: Country Rock

Words and Music by Buddy Brock
and Aaron Tippin

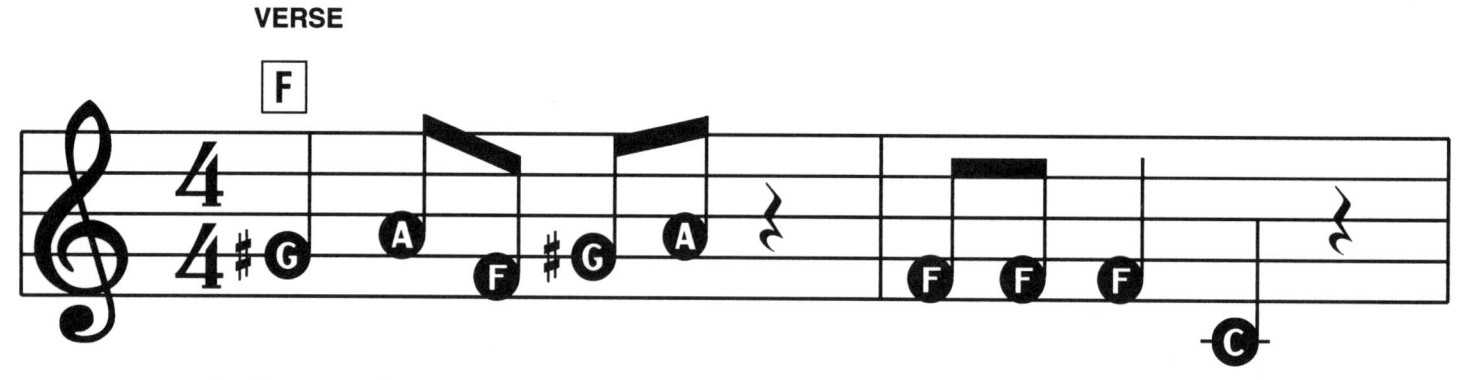

VERSE

1. Some-times she runs, _____ some-times she don't.
2. *(See additional lyrics)*

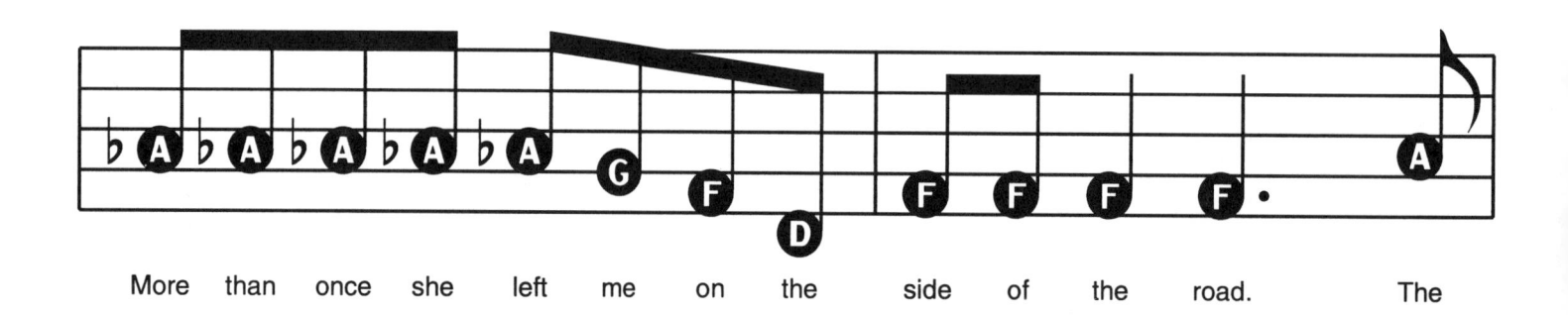

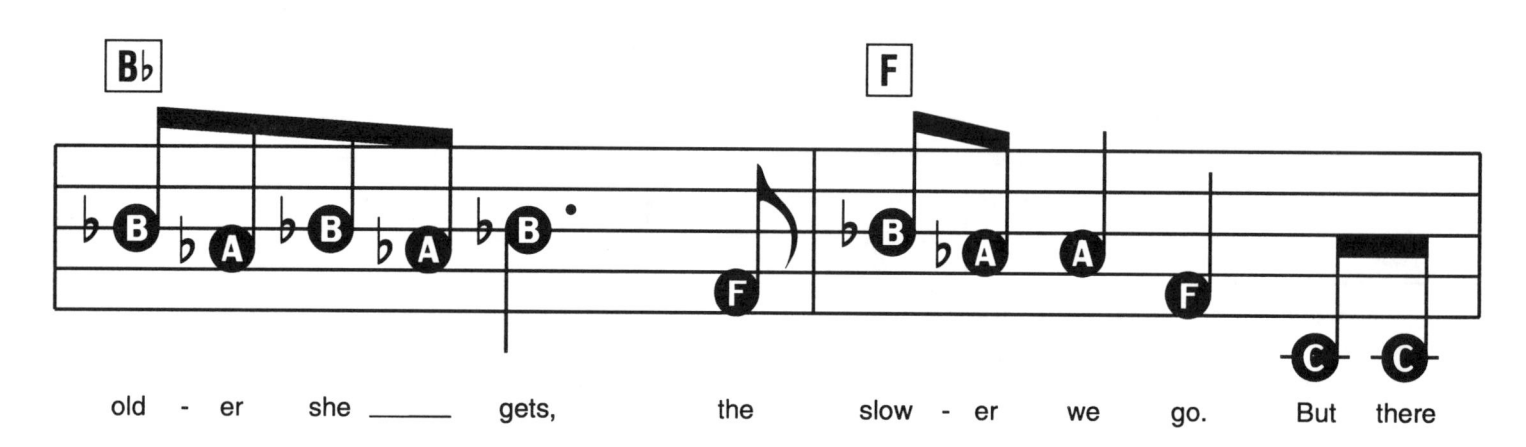

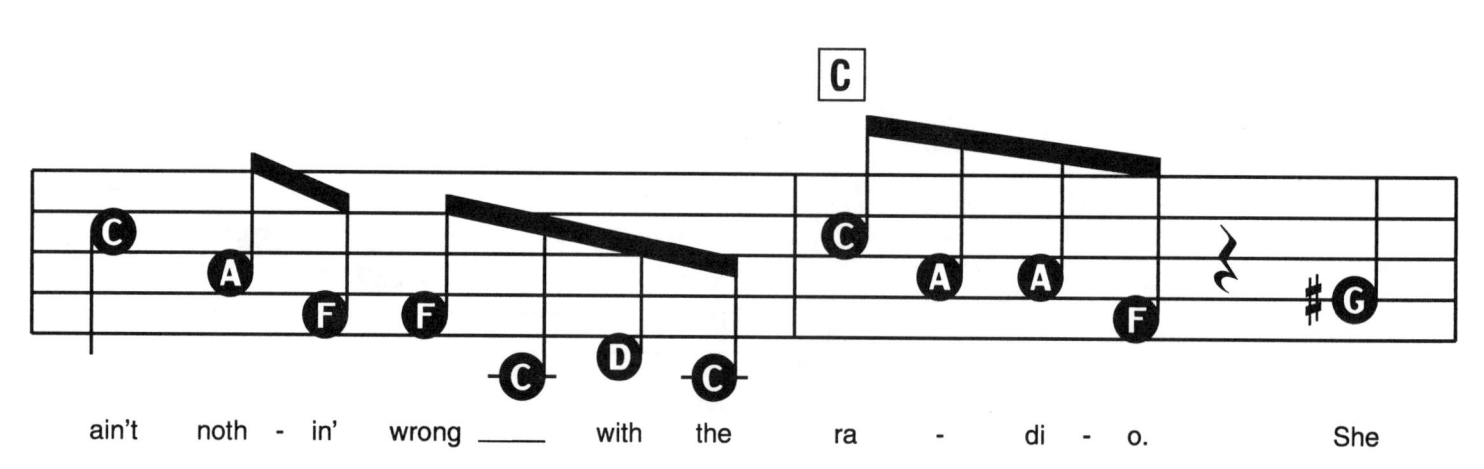

More than once she left me on the side of the road. The

old-er she _____ gets, the slow-er we go. But there

ain't noth-in' wrong _____ with the ra-di-o. She

Copyright © 1991 ACUFF-ROSE MUSIC, INC. (BMI), 65 Music Square West, Nashville, TN 37203
International Copyright Secured   All Rights Reserved

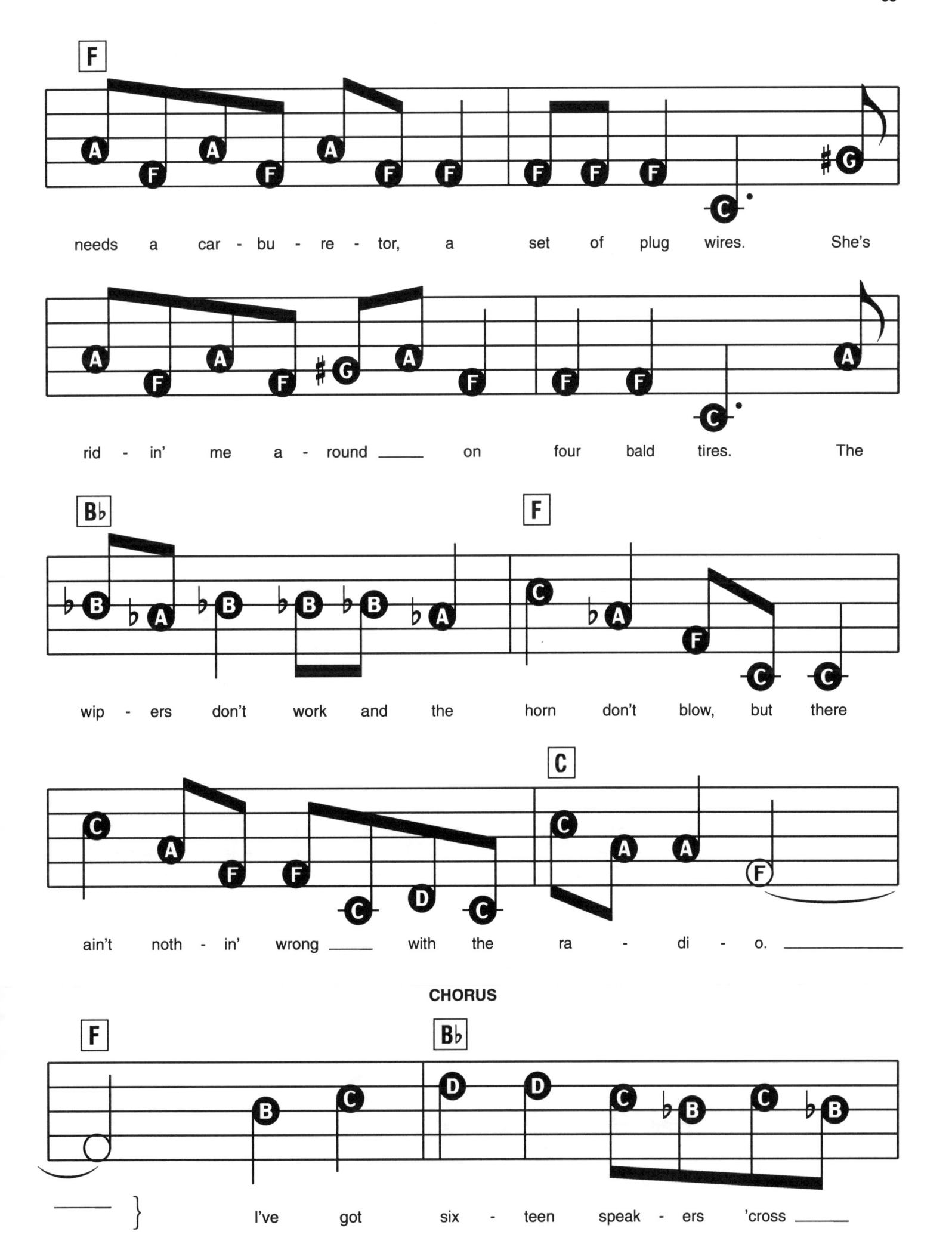

needs a car - bu - re - tor, a set of plug wires. She's
rid - in' me a - round ____ on four bald tires. The
wip - ers don't work and the horn don't blow, but there
ain't noth - in' wrong ____ with the ra - di - o. ____

CHORUS

____ I've got six - teen speak - ers 'cross ____

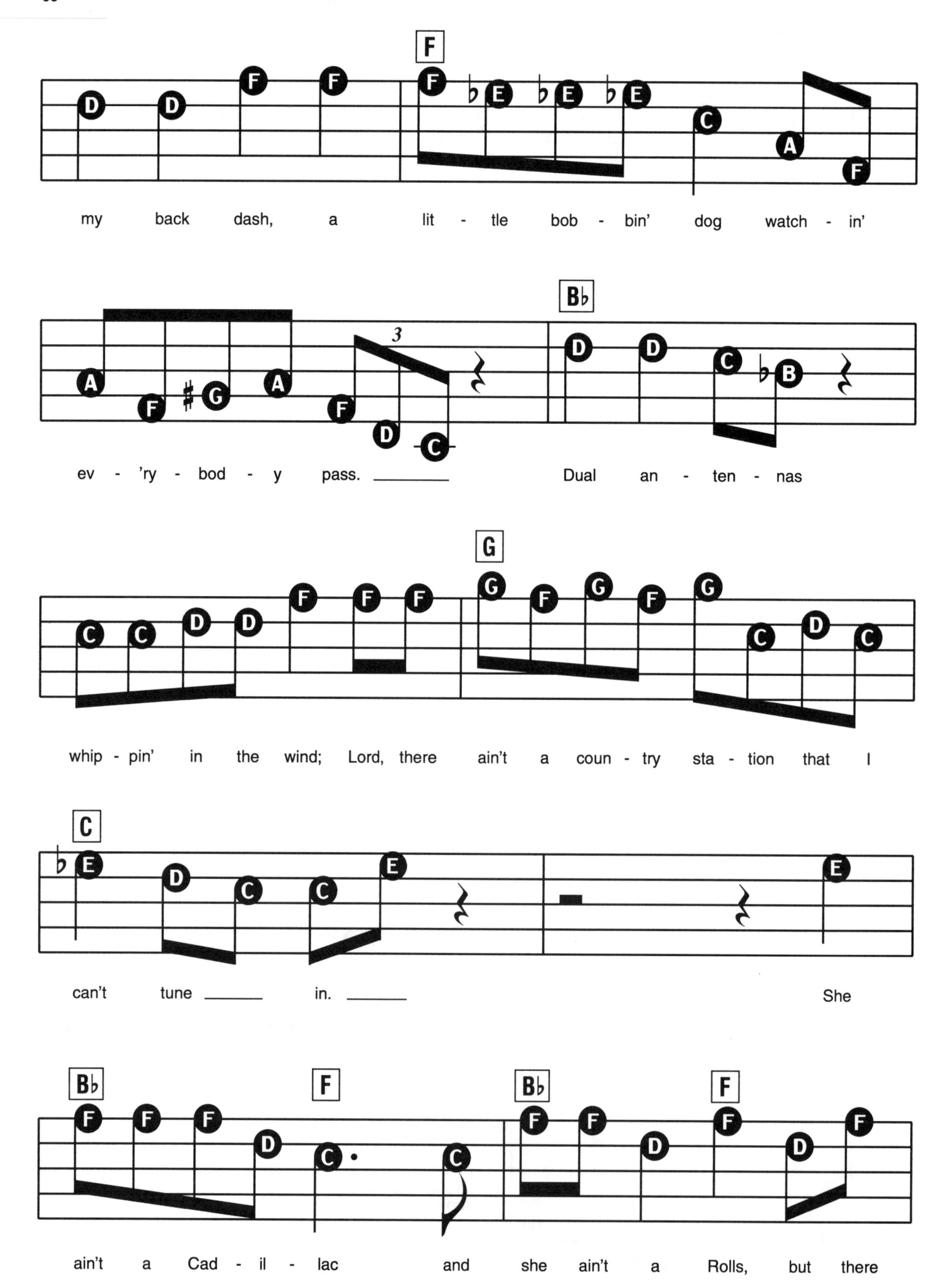

my back dash, a little bobbin' dog watchin' ev-'ry-bod-y pass. Dual an-ten-nas whip-pin' in the wind; Lord, there ain't a coun-try sta-tion that I can't tune in. She ain't a Cad-il-lac and she ain't a Rolls, but there ain't noth-in' wrong ___ with the ra - di - o.

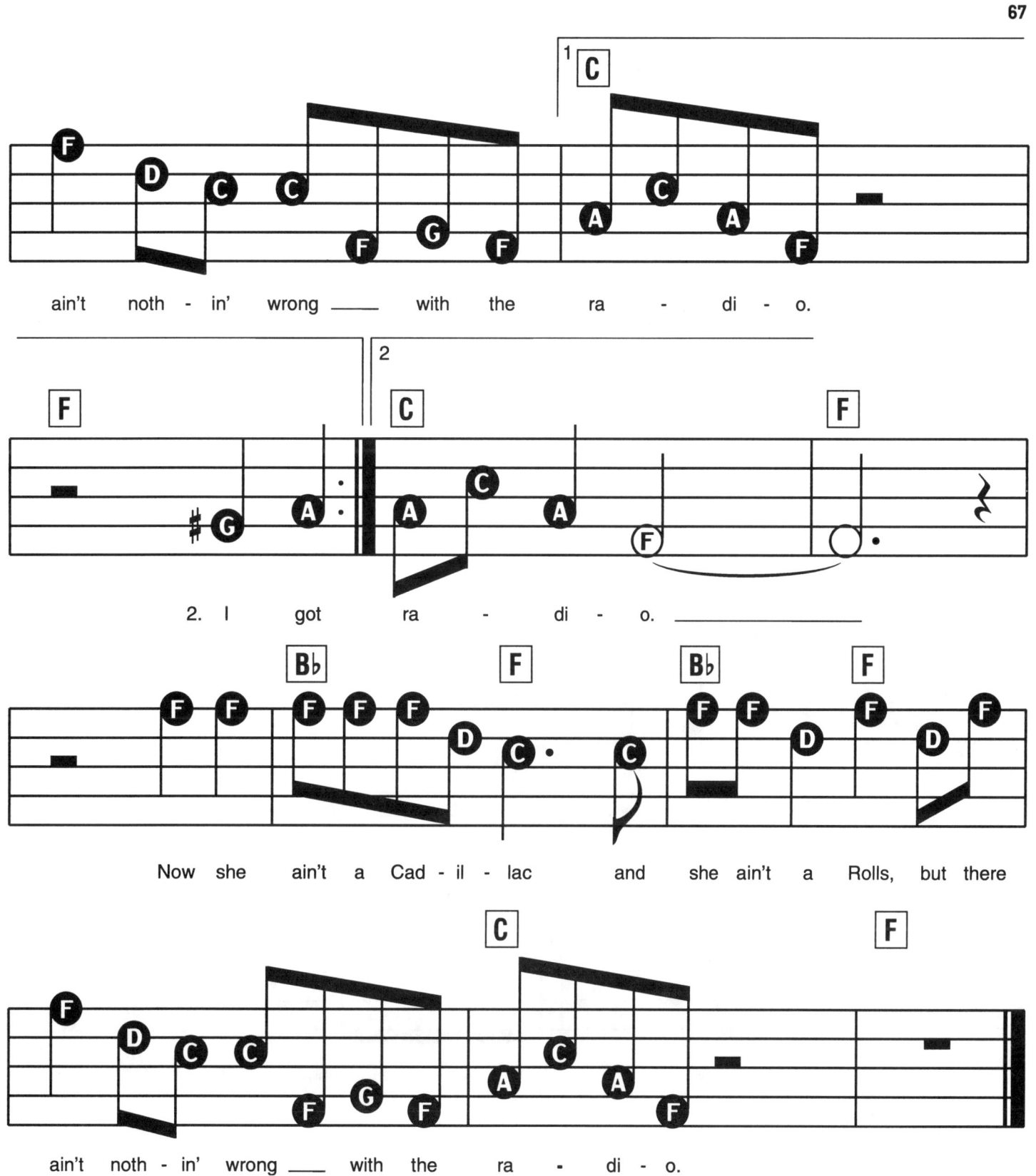

2. I got ra - di - o. ___

Now she ain't a Cad - il - lac and she ain't a Rolls, but there

ain't noth-in' wrong ___ with the ra - di - o.

Additional Lyrics

2. I got stopped by a cop late last night,
   Out of date tags and no tail lights.
   He said, "I ought to run you in but I'm lettin' you go
   Because there ain't nothin' wrong with your radio."
   I've got the best lookin' gal in my whole town.
   I asked her last time that I took her out,
   "Honey, tell me what it is that makes you love me so."
   She said, "There ain't nothin' wrong with your radio."
   To Chorus:

Straight Tequila Night

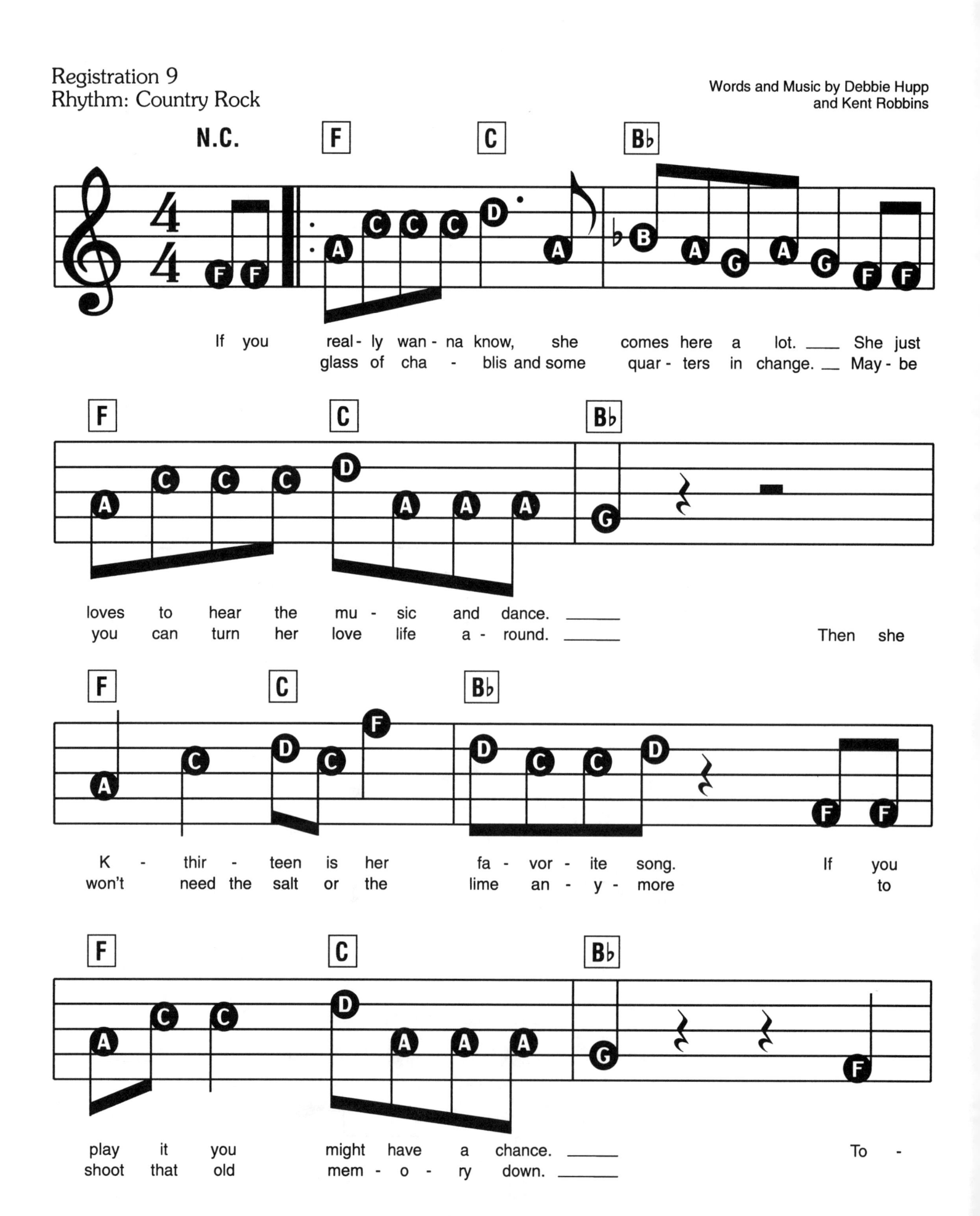

Registration 9
Rhythm: Country Rock

Words and Music by Debbie Hupp
and Kent Robbins

If you real-ly wan-na know, she comes here a lot. ___ She just
glass of cha - blis and some quar-ters in change. ___ May-be

loves to hear the mu-sic and dance. ___
you can turn her love life a - round. ___ Then she

K - thir - teen is her fa - vor - ite song. If you
won't need the salt or the lime an - y - more to

play it you might have a chance. ___
shoot that old mem - o - ry down. ___ To -

Copyright © 1991 Dixie Stars Music, Irving Music, Inc. and Colter Bay Music
International Copyright Secured   All Rights Reserved

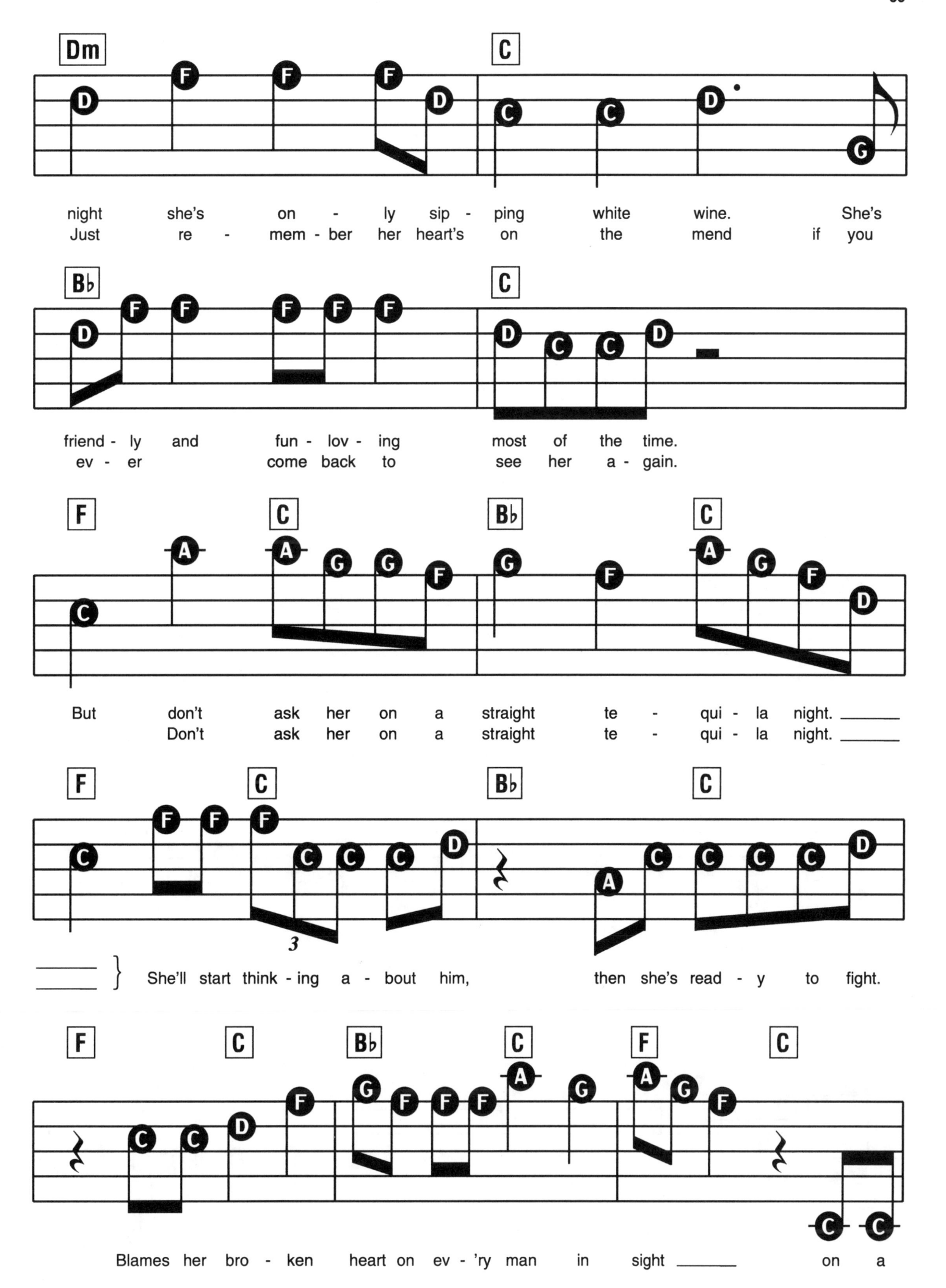

night she's on-ly sip-ping white wine. She's
Just re-mem-ber her heart's on the mend if you

friend-ly and fun-lov-ing most of the time.
ev-er come back to see her a-gain.

But don't ask her on a straight te-qui-la night. _____
Don't ask her on a straight te-qui-la night. _____

_____ She'll start think-ing a-bout him, then she's read-y to fight.

Blames her bro-ken heart on ev-'ry man in sight _____ on a

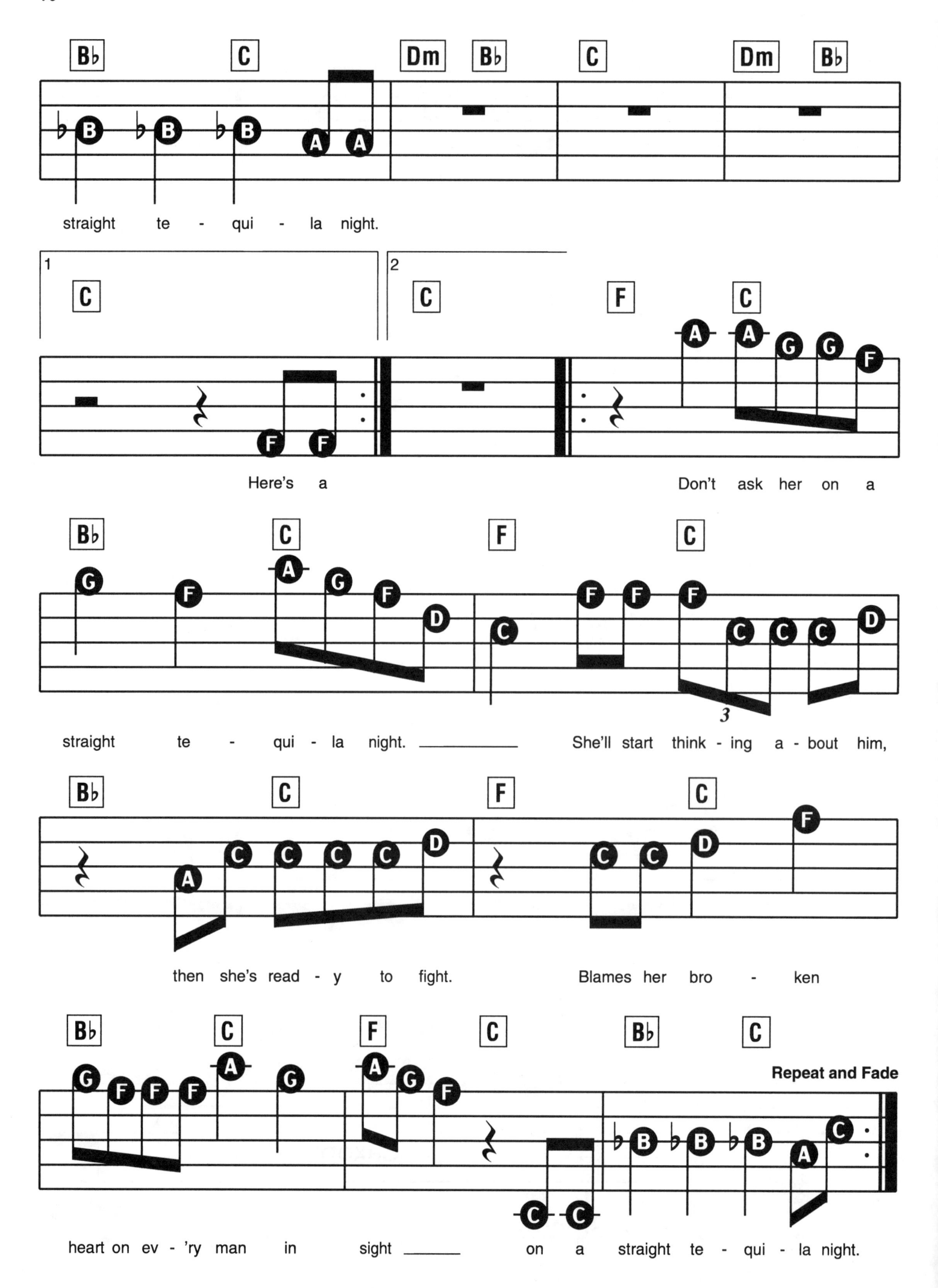

straight te - qui - la night.

Here's a   Don't ask her on a

straight te - qui - la night. _____ She'll start think-ing a-bout him,

then she's read-y to fight.   Blames her bro-ken

Repeat and Fade

heart on ev-'ry man in sight _____ on a straight te-qui-la night.

E-Z Play Today Registration Guide

- Match the Registration number on the song to the corresponding numbered category below. Select and activate an instrumental sound available on your instrument.
- Choose an automatic rhythm appropriate to the mood and style of the song. (Consult your Owner's Guide for proper operation of automatic rhythm features.)
- Adjust the tempo and volume controls to comfortable settings.

Registration

1	Flute, Pan Flute, Jazz Flute
2	Clarinet, Organ
3	Violin, Strings
4	Brass, Trumpet, Bass
5	Synth Ensemble, Accordion, Brass
6	Pipe Organ, Harpsichord
7	Jazz Organ, Vibraphone, Vibes, Electric Piano, Jazz Guitar
8	Piano, Electric Piano
9	Trumpet, Trombone, Clarinet, Saxophone, Oboe
10	Violin, Cello, Strings